D0523351

"The Complete Lean Enterprise is an excellent tool to guide the enterprising manager to a new lean process solution. The step-by-step instructions are easy for the beginner to follow, and the lean examples, team exercises, and mapping tips add a credible voice of experience to the manuscript. And, best of all, 'It works!' "

Kent Sears, Vice President
Manufacturing Processes and Lean Implementation
General Motors Corporation

"Keyte and Locher have provided a valuable contribution for identifying strategic operational value streams for administrative and office processes. They demonstrate that the next generation of waste identification and elimination is in the business support functions."

Dr. Ross E. Robson
Executive Director
Shingo Prize for Excellence in Manufacturing
Utah State University

The Complete Lean Enterprise

Value Stream Mapping for Administrative and Office Processes

Beau Keyte and Drew Locher

Productivity Press

New York

© 2004 by Productivity Press, a division of Kraus Productivity Organization, Ltd.

All rights reserved. No part of this book may be reproduced or utilized in any form or by any means, electronic or mechanical, including photocopying, recording, or by any information storage and retrieval system, without permission in writing from the publisher.

Most Productivity Press books are available at quantity discounts when purchased in bulk. For more information contact our Customer Service Department (888-319-5852). Address all other inquires to:

Productivity Press
444 Park Avenue South, 7th floor
New York, NY 10016
United States of America
Telephone 212-686-5900
Fax: 212-686-5411
E-mail: info@productivitypress.com

Cover design by Gary Raggaglia
Text Design and Page composition by William H. Brunson Typography Services
Art creation by Lorraine Millard
Printed and bound by Malloy Lithographing in the United States of America

Library of Congress Cataloging-in-Publication Data

Keyte, Beau.
    The complete lean enterprise : value stream mapping for administrative and office processes / Beau Keyte and Drew Locher.
        p. cm.
    Includes bibliographical references and index.
    ISBN 1-56327-301-2 (alk. paper)
    1. Organizational effectiveness.   2. Industrial efficiency.   3. Office management—Cost control.   4. Industrial management—Cost effectiveness.   5. Value added.   I. Keyte, Beau and Locher, Drew.
II. Title.

HD58.9.K455   2004
651.3—dc22

2004009539

09 08 07   10 9 8 7 6

Dedication

*To my dad and Debi, whose constant love and support have
carried me through these years and allowed me to chase my dream.
And, thanks to the great people who have worked with us to
create fundamental changes in their organizations.*

—Beau Keyte

*To Eileen, without your love and support I could never succeed.
Thanks to all of the companies with whom I have worked—
you are the true innovators.*

—Drew Locher

Whenever there is a product for a customer, there is a value stream. The challenge lies in seeing it.

—Mike Rother and John Shook, *Learning to See*

When you have learned to see value streams in individual facilities, it's time to see and then optimize entire value streams from raw material to the customer.

—Dan Jones and Jim Womack, *Seeing the Whole*

When you have learned to see the "raw material to the customer" value stream, it's time to see, challenge, and optimize how the rest of the enterprise supports the core value stream.

—Beau Keyte and Drew Locher

CONTENTS

FOREWORD

An alternate title for this book could be *Waste in the Office: The Final Lean Frontier.* Beau Keyte and Drew Locher have accomplished an ambitious task—one that can benefit anyone concerned with creating maximum value for customers with as little waste as possible.

How much waste is there in an enterprise? Stated differently, what percent of activities undertaken by each of us every day actually contribute toward the creation of value for our customers? Quantifying waste on such a scale would, no doubt, be an endeavor that would in itself constitute waste, and a massive amount of it at that. Certainly, when we ask how many of our actions directly provide value for our customers, the answer is loud and clear: painfully little.

Since the publications of *The Machine That Changed the World* in 1989 and *Lean Thinking* in 1997, hundreds if not thousands of firms around the world have launched initiatives to eliminate waste in their operations. Many of those efforts have been fantastically successful while others have proved frustratingly slow or even ineffective. Either way, the great majority of those efforts have been aimed at the plant floor or other direct operations. Yet, as firms proceed with improvement activities on the plant floor they encounter the inevitable reality that fundamental change—even on the plant floor—ultimately requires the involvement and support of the entire enterprise.

Beau and Drew tell us that 90 percent of waste eliminating opportunities in manufacturing firms is to be found outside of direct manufacturing operations, away from the plant floor. And, not only is that amount of waste tremendous in scope, even more troublesome is the fact that "office waste" is extremely difficult to eliminate due to the simple fact that it is also extremely difficult to *see*.

That is where Beau and Drew come in with this book. Just as *Learning To See* introduced a fresh set of lenses through which to view the manufacturing world, Beau and Drew expand the use of the now-proven Value Stream Mapping (VSM) tool to indirect, support operations, the locations and sources of so much waste in organizations. VSM as introduced by Beau and Drew seeks to enable users to see administrative waste, identify its sources, and develop a future state that eliminates it so that scarce resources can then be focused on those activities truly necessary to create value.

You could find no two more experienced guides for this journey than the well-traveled Beau and Drew. Beau and Drew have been teaming together to teach workshops on the topic for several years, at the Lean Enterprise Institute, the NIST MEP, at universities and for corporations large and small. Their collective experience covers a wide range of enterprises and industries: automotive OEMs and suppliers, aerospace, electronics, consumer perishables, information technology, health care, and more.

So, grab your pencils and paper and your walking shoes. The opportunities that present themselves as you learn to peel away the obscurity of administrative work will be tremendous. It's time to get started.

Dan Jones
Ross-on-Wye, England

John Shook
Ann Arbor, Michigan, USA

ACKNOWLEDGEMENTS

To everyone at the Lean Enterprise Institute and the Lean Enterprise Academy for giving us the opportunity, time and support in testing these new waters. Special thanks to John Shook and Mike Rother for paving the way.

We began our efforts with a "good" manuscript, and were helped over the past several months in the creation of a "great" book. Several editors, graphic designers, and reviewers helped us get there including: Gary Peurasaari, Nancy Heller, Bob Cooper, Mike Sinocchi, John Shook, Dan Jones, Jeff Durham, and John Louchheim.

INTRODUCTION

A highly revered ex-Toyota consultant recently stated that most manufacturers seem focused on achieving a 35 to 40 percent productivity gain over three to five years as a measure of success in their current lean efforts. He went on to say that manufacturers should be actually focusing on a 400 percent improvement in productivity over 10 years to achieve the path to becoming lean. Why is there such a large disparity in measuring success?

One way of looking at this 360 percent gap is to recognize that most lean initiatives only focus on applying lean principles on the shop floor where the opportunity to increase productivity might indeed be limited to 35 to 40 percent over several years. We have observed that much of the untapped potential for improvement in an enterprise's productivity lies off the shop floor in nonproduction areas where the enterprise has yet to understand or embrace lean thinking and principles.

When we point this fact out to companies, there is ready agreement that when it comes to incorporating lean they tend to ignore nonproduction areas. One of the major difficulties companies have in applying lean principles to nonproduction operations is their inability to apply systems thinking in identifying value, waste, and flow in the office. Companies can readily use an excellent book like *Learning to See* (1999), by Mike Rother and John Shook, to use value stream mapping to visualize their value stream from raw material to the customer on the shop floor, but the mapping tool and principles do not appear to be easily transferable to their nonproduction order-to-cash processes.

We've been successful in applying lean tools and techniques in offices and service industries since 1992 and quickly embraced *Learning to See* as a standard for value stream mapping when it was published several years ago. However, it was apparent that the tool needed to be adapted to the applications and issues we have seen when implementing lean transformations within the office. The state of the office is different than the state of the shop floor in most organizations. While many new ideas, including lean concepts, have been introduced on the shop floor, new ideas in the office appear to be limited to expensive information systems and reorganizations; neither of these solutions have made a big dent in the competitiveness of enterprises. As a result, we developed this workbook to raise the consciousness of the people responsible for nonproduction processes, and to challenge how they support the organization. In addition, we demonstrate how to see the organization within a systems perspective. To accomplish this, we've supplemented the value stream mapping perspective and technique with:

- Discussions on office waste (Chapter 3).

- Definitions and discussions of office performance metrics (Chapter 5).

- Functional lean perspectives (Chapter 7).

- Case studies representing two levels (altitudes) of mapping. (The first level is the main case study, discussed throughout the text. The one discussed in the Appendix represents the second level.)

- Examples of companies applying lean thinking in the office throughout the book.

It is our hope that this workbook can provide companies with the confidence needed to understand the value created in their organizations, as well as give them the ability to leverage lean concepts in both production and nonproduction areas. This will enable them to meet their business objectives and pursue the ultimate goal of becoming a lean enterprise—the ideal lean state.

The Complete Lean Enterprise

Value Stream Mapping for Administrative and Office Processes

CHAPTER 1

Applying Value Stream Mapping Throughout the Enterprise

It may surprise some people, but all of the lean concepts typically applied to the production processes of an organization also apply to nonproduction and administrative processes. The challenge is being creative enough to figure out how to best use them in particular areas of the company in order to realize meaningful benefits. In their landmark book *Lean Thinking* (1996), James Womack and Daniel Jones define a value stream as follows:

The set of all specific actions required to bring a specific product through the three critical management tasks of any business:

1. Problem solving (e.g., design).

2. Information management (e.g., order processing and other non-production activities).

3. Physical transformation (e.g., converting raw materials to finished product).

Management of these value streams—value stream management—involves a process for measuring, understanding, and improving the flow and interactions of all the associated tasks to keep the cost, service, and quality of a company's products and services as competitive as possible. More important, value stream management sets the stage to implement a lean transformation throughout the whole enterprise and keeps an organization from falling back into the traditional suboptimal approach of improving departmental-level efficiencies. A basic but powerful two-dimensional tool of Value Stream Management is value stream mapping. It documents and directs a lean transformation from a systems, or big picture, perspective.

Though value stream mapping can identify continued opportunities to enhance value, eliminate waste, and improve flow, it is not the end, but the beginning of the journey in value stream management. In Deming terms, it is the "P" in the PDCA (plan-do-check-act) cycle (see Figure 1-1). It allows a company to document, measure, and analyze a complex set of relationships as well as to plot a course to create an improved operating strategy and organizational design. Once the company agrees on the design, it is ready to apply the appropriate lean tools and techniques to improve the performance of the overall value stream. The company manages this value stream by continuing to challenge and redesign its level of cost, quality, and service as perceived by the customer in the markets it serves.

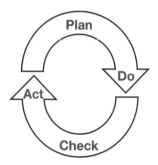

Figure 1-1. PDCA Cycle

The six steps an organization can use to implement Value Stream Management are highlighted in the box below. This workbook focuses on steps 3 through 5. Other sources such as "Lean Thinking" provide valuable insight to steps 1, 2, and 6.

Steps for Success in Value Stream Management

1. Identify the need to change the organization from top-level management to one driven by strategic needs.

2. Understand and support the basics of a lean strategy at all levels of the organization.

3. Identify and select a value stream manager for each major value stream.

4. Create lean metrics that drive and support lean behavior in creating value, eliminating waste, and monitoring the financial and operating course to strategic success.

5. Implement future-state value stream designs.

6. Communicate top-level management's continued leadership in focusing on the organization's pursuit of a competitive operating strategy by using lean tools and techniques throughout the enterprise.

Applying Value Stream Mapping to Nonproduction Areas

Many companies have made considerable progress on Womack and Jones's third critical management task—*physical transformation* on the shop floor. However, they have encountered tremendous difficulties when addressing *problem solving* and *information management* in the nonproduction areas. Companies struggling to apply lean principles to nonproduction areas often approach us with these common questions:

- How can takt time and takt image be applied to administrative areas?

- Are there really opportunities to apply the concepts of continuous flow and pull?

- What about mix and volume leveling: Don't these concepts only apply to the production processes?

- What meaningful lean metrics can you use to understand the value stream performance?

Clearly, the issue at hand is that many companies have little experience in applying lean concepts to nonproduction areas. Further, there are few examples from which companies can learn. The intent of this workbook is to provide a basis of understanding as well as the necessary tools to initiate Value Stream Management for Womack and Jones's second task, *information management*. Our primary focus is to teach the mapping techniques for the order-to-cash value stream, which covers all value streams typically associated with the nonproduction areas or the administrative and office activities of an enterprise.

In our travels, people have referred to nonproduction activities as order-to-cash, administrative, and office value streams. For the sake of simplicity, we call them office value streams (see Figure 1-2). Simply defined, an office value stream is the series of activities or processes supporting the daily production needs of the enterprise. Many, but not all, directly affect the information flow to the shop floor. These value streams include all the activities, both those that create value and those that add no value, required to complete the service defined by the value stream. Examples of office value streams range from quoting new business, to the creation of invoices, to the receipt of payment from customers. For those readers concerned with the *problem solving*

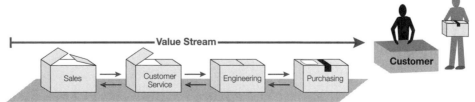

Figure 1-2. Office Value Stream

(concept-to-launch) value stream, these techniques are also directly transferable to many product design and development activities.

Purpose of the Case Study

In this workbook, we use the case study of ABC Design Company to roll out value stream mapping techniques that will be familiar to those that have gone through this process for the shop floor, but will be unique to all in their application to information management. Beginning with the lean concepts applied to the production area, we will illustrate the step-by-step application of the principles of value stream mapping in developing ABC Design's current and future-state value stream map representing the remainder of the enterprise. This exercise should give a bird's eye view of ABC Design's transformation as it goes through the process of first developing a current state map, then a future state map, and then devising its work plan. Finally, in the Appendix we drill down into the organization and map only the areas associated with order entry and engineering drawings. The significance of this drill down is to help the organization develop improved processes within the framework of an enterprise future state. In other words, once the organization knows what direction it should be taking as a whole, it's time to understand how the various aspects of the enterprise should redesign their work to be in line with the big picture or systems perspective.

CHAPTER 2

Getting Started: Mapping Office Value Streams

Companies can use the value stream mapping tool in the office the same way they use it on the shop floor. The mapping tool is designed to capture the way work is organized and progresses throughout an organization (or series of organizations) to enable management to:

- Visualize the process.

- Point to problems.

- Focus the direction of its lean transformation.

However, there are some distinct differences between the office and the shop floor. In the office, *material flow* is the actual flow of data, either on paper or electronically, that takes place to complete a service. *Information flow*—the scheduling or sequencing mechanism that triggers the next task—occurs in both production systems and office systems. However, unlike production systems, information flows in office systems are loosely structured and use informal scheduling, which makes it difficult to identify and map their values streams. Furthermore, administrative departments typically support several value streams, making it even more difficult to document the workflow of each individual value stream. For example, customer service might be involved in quoting, order entry, invoicing, and telemarketing. In addition, these office value streams are rarely contained in a single department.

The fact is, companies typically view administrative departments such as human resources, finance, engineering, and purchasing as independently contributing to the success of the company. They do not see the interaction and integration of the work activities involving multiple functions and departments. It is no wonder that companies have difficultly grasping the concepts of a new value stream design for the office.

Lean Note: The lean term *information management* refers to the critical management task of managing the paperwork that is involved in supporting the organization, such as order processing. This is not to be confused with *information flow*, which technically refers to the trigger that signals a process (or someone) to do actual work.

A company can moderate the inherent challenges of Value Stream Management in the office by identifying and redesigning one or two value streams to begin with, then adding more as it continues its lean transformation. When mapping the shop floor, a cross-functional team follows the path of a product and draws a visual representation of what they observe. For the office, it is typically a service, which may or may not result in a tangible product, that is the basis of the mapping observations. The teams map the tasks, the information flow, and the performance of each of these service tasks. Then the team members ask a set of prescriptive questions to challenge the present design of the value stream and draw a new—future—design with enhanced value, better flow, and less waste. As the company continues to address its value streams, it will become easier to see value and waste to design more effective value streams and enterprises.

As we move forward, you will see how companies use office value stream mapping in their lean transformation to tackle strategic business issues and organizational challenges, for example, such activities as improving handoffs of paperwork and information, changing new office information systems, redefining roles and responsibilities in support of new production strategies, improving coordination among field offices, and moving or merging companies. Companies can also use value stream mapping to expand an office value stream into customer organizations to get statistical trends on sales and new product requirements, and into supplier organizations to get production support.

Understanding Value Stream Mapping Basics

The purpose of value stream mapping is to assist a management team in visualizing and communicating not only how its organization acts today, but also how it should act in the future to influence the cost, service, and quality of its products and services. In fact, value stream maps are the essential lean tools that enable and facilitate value stream management, as well as the key management tools for continuing to implement and manage new value streams. This is why value stream mapping is the first and most important tool for establishing the direction and focus of a lean transformation. The following sections provide an overview of how mapping works.

Service Family. Each mapping effort involves a redesign of a specific process or set of processes we call a service family. This service family represents all the work and transactions the team seeks to change using the value-stream mapping tool (see Figure 2-1). Mapping begins with identifying these service families.

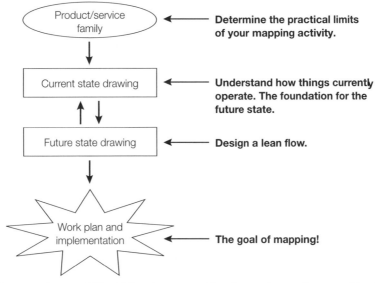

Figure 2-1. Steps for Mapping an Office Value Stream and Implementing an Improved Design (derived from *Learning to See,* V1.2, p.9)

Current State. Once the mapping team has established the product/service family, it draws a *current state map*. The current state map is the beginning point of the enterprise transformation: it represents how the company organizes and progresses work today—its baseline condition. The map itself solves no problems. Rather its purpose is to gather information on a process quickly and visually to point to problems in the company's work streams. This effort should take the mapping team about a day to complete.

Future State. The *future state map* focuses the direction of a new design for the value stream and its intended performance at a point in a lean transformation. Typically, the mapping team's current and future state mapping events influence each other. That is, many of the team's ideas for the future value stream begin during the current state drawing effort as the team challenges the structure of the current value stream. Likewise, the team often finds the need to collect extra current state information as they design the future state map. The mapping team should also complete the future state map in about a day.

Future states can describe how the value stream should operate over a wide range of timelines. The mapping team might want to draw a picture of how the value stream should operate at the end of three months, or at the end of one year. This time frame is a critical decision: the longer the time frame, the more changes the company can incorporate within the future state design. But, if the timeline is too long, organizations can get frustrated waiting for documented change. It's best to keep the first future state design within a three- to six-month time frame for implementation. This gives a company the ability to complete a few significant projects in a timely manner.

> *Mapping Tip:* Companies rarely design a future state that requires more than 12 months to implement, since business conditions can change. Therefore, companies must view the future state drawing as an iterative working document that they can use to drive an organization's continuous improvement effort.

Work Plan. The final and most important step is for the mapping team to develop a detailed work plan for the company to implement. The mapping effort is simply a tool: implementing the work plan is the key. The work plan should describe the required improvement projects that are necessary for realizing the future state—or what lean practitioners refer to as *kaizens*. *Kaizen* is a Japanese term for stressing *continuous incremental improvements* to achieve the lean goal of creating more value in the organization, as well as striving for perfection. The mapping team identifies these kaizens in the development of the future state map. This detailed work plan is a critical success factor for Value Stream Management because it provides the management team with sufficient detail to track, manage, and react to the progress of the implementation effort. Once the team develops a future state map, it should complete the work plan in about a day.

Scoping the Selected Value Stream and Choosing the Mapping Team

Before the team begins mapping, preparation, or scoping, activities are necessary to ensure a successful event. The following activities help management set up the company's office value stream mapping events:

- Select a service family.
- Determine a manageable boundary.
- Choose the value stream team.

Each of these is discussed in the following sections.

Select a Service Family

Whether the mandate of the company is to redesign an entire enterprise or a specific set of functions or activities within the enterprise, the team must first define the company's product or service families. A family is a group of products and/or services that share *similar* processing steps—they do not have to be identical to each other. Although most office work is service related, in some cases true office products exist, such as production documentation, repair manuals, and engineering drawings.

One of the first things the team should do is develop a matrix of products or services and processing steps to facilitate discussions of product and service families (see Figure 2-2). The team begins this discussion by identifying the company's product and service families from the customer (internal or external) perspective of the value stream. In the case of order processing, the team might ask whether customer needs differ based on the type of product that the customer is ordering—that is, do the processing steps substantially differ based on the type of order it is? Perhaps the company currently treats all orders the same, while it might be more effective to treat them differently because the customer needs, or the processing steps, are markedly different.

Product	Processing Steps			
	Estimate/Quote	Design/Configure	Enter order	Generate job packet
Model A			X	X
Model B			X	X
Model C	X	X	X	X
Model D	X	X	X	X

Figure 2-2. Matrix of Products/Services and Processing Steps

Upon examining the matrix, it is clear that there are really two families of products: the standard (i.e., those that already exist—Models A and B in Figure 2-2) and the nonstandard (i.e., those that require some level of estimating and design activity—Models C and D in the figure). In addition, the customer needs might be different; for example, standard products might require a one-week lead time, while four weeks is acceptable for nonstandard products.

In another example, many companies use the same processing steps for all engineering changes, resulting in very long lead times for very simple changes. In this case, it would be best to develop a matrix showing the relationships between the engineering changes, since there are arguably four types of engineering changes represented by multiple families (see Figure 2-3).

Engineering Change Type	Processing Steps			
	Change drawing	Change bill of material	Analyze inventory impact	Analyze financial impact
"A"	X			
"B"	X	X		
"C"	X	X	X	
"D"	X	X	X	X

Figure 2-3. Matrix of Products/Services and Processing Steps Showing Relationships of Engineering Changes

---

TEAM DISCUSSION

The team's challenge is to isolate the different families to distinguish the needs of the customer and the purposes of the transactions for each of the families.

It is particularly important to make these distinctions when the team is developing a future state. It may be desirable for a company to establish multiple future states (i.e., processes or systems) for multiple product or service families. Under these circumstances, the team would redesign each value stream to meet the specific needs of the customer in the most effective way (i.e., minimal lead time, minimal cost).

Determine a Manageable Boundary

Once the team identifies a product or service family it is ready to decide upon an appropriate level of detail. There are four mapping levels for a product or service family (see Figure 2-4). These levels cover mapping from the micro to macro perspective. The macro perspective is gained through the "across companies" level, which visualizes how different entities in the supply chain coordinate the paperwork to support a final consumer of their product. The "single or multiple sites" level visualizes how one or more sites within a single company coordinate the paperwork to support a customer outside the organization, and is used to identify the main areas to begin a lean transformation. This level is demonstrated in our main case study. The "cross functional" level is used once there is a decision to focus a value stream redesign within a specific process of a company (e.g., new product development, product sourcing, invoicing). This level is demonstrated in the appendix case study. The "process level" can be coined the "cubicle level," as it is used for a detailed redesign of a specific task within a process. Typically, a team begins mapping at a site or multisite level and then quickly moves to a cross-functional level. No matter what level the team begins at, it is imperative that the value stream mapping effort provide enough information to point to problems, as well as focus the direction needed for the selected service family.

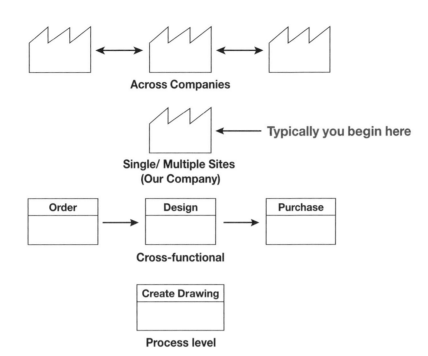

Figure 2-4. Levels of Mapping the Value Stream for a Product or Service Family (derived from *Learning to See,* V1.2, p. 13)

For site-level office value stream mapping, the team should include all primary business functions in an enterprise, such as:

- Sales and marketing.

- Order processing.

- Design.

- Inventory control.

- Purchasing.

- Production control and scheduling.

- Accounts payable.

- Invoicing and accounts receivable.

Lean Note: It is critical that companies obtain (and maintain!) the overall big-picture view of the organization *before* initiating process-level improvement efforts. The big picture typically focuses on those functions that impact the ability of the company to deliver products to the customers. A company in a lean transformation should only focus on other necessary support functions such as human resources, information systems, legal, finance, etc. *after* understanding the interactions between the primary business functions and the manufacturing operation.

While the site level map may provide enough information to begin the design of a lean enterprise, it might not provide enough documentation for complex organizations to develop a sufficiently detailed future state map and implementation plan. In a large organization or one in which the service family has many tasks (which can be determined by finding out where one-piece flow ends), it might make sense to quickly move from the completed site level map to a cross-functional level, to map and implement a new value stream design. For example, a quoting process requiring several people completing dozens of tasks spanning many days or weeks would require a cross-functional level map to provide enough understanding to design a future state.

Choose the Value Stream Team

The team designing the new value stream should be made up of those managers representing functions that support the value stream under study. Ample time must be given for team members to be educated in lean thinking and value stream mapping. The best scenario would be to have the team involved in the key preparation activities discussed earlier in this chapter. The team should consist of a value stream manager and supporting cross-functional team members.

Value Stream Manager. The value stream manager is the person assigned to lead the future state design implementation across functional and departmental boundaries. This person can also be responsible for the ongoing success of Value Stream Management. The value stream manager must be knowledgeable, respected within the organization, and have good facilitating and coaching skills (see Figure 2-5). It is imperative that management not only select a qualified value stream manager, but also create the appropriate work environment for the selected person to perform in. One problem that frequently occurs is when management assigns an employee to be a part-time value stream manager while his or her "regular"

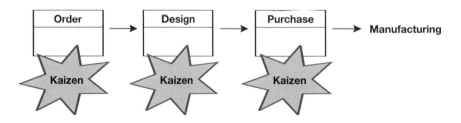

Figure 2-5. The Value Stream Manager—Don't Begin the Effort Without One! (derived from *Learning to See,* V1.2, p.7)

job still reports to the department head of the very department being mapped. This creates a potential for the department head to assert his or her "command and control" and trump any changes the value stream manager is trying to oversee. To avoid this conflict of interest, management must provide the value stream manager with the political support necessary for the difficult tasks required to enable change. In other words, it may be necessary to change reporting relationships to give the value stream manager the resources and authority necessary to implement the future state successfully.

Cross-Functional Team Members. The value stream team members are responsible for completing the value stream analysis, which includes current and future state mapping, and assisting the value stream manager in implementing the new value stream design. Depending on the scope (or whether it is a site or cross-functional level map), management needs to select a cross-functional team with representatives from each of the primary functional areas impacted by the selected value stream. In total, six to eight members may be directly involved in the actual mapping events. Other members may be involved on an as-needed basis.

Once the team is established, the members must gain an understanding of some of the specific kinds of waste that occur in offices; these are discussed in the next chapter.

CHAPTER 3

Identifying Office Waste

Many companies have been lulled into thinking that a lean transformation is limited to changes on the manufacturing floor for the simple reason that they have a difficult time differentiating value from waste and implementing improvements in administrative areas. Though companies have made commendable strides in production system improvements, many have excluded critical office processes from the shop floor value stream map, rendering an incomplete enterprise map. This incomplete picture diminishes the usefulness of the map because companies will fail to "see the enterprise" and the significant opportunities for enhancing value and eliminating waste that exist in the nonproduction areas.

Equally important, a company may overlook the root causes for the various wastes observed in the shop floor map that often reside in support processes. We often use the expression "the information flow is the fuel that drives the material flow." If these support processes are left unchanged, the improvement efforts in the production processes are often undercut, leaving unrecognized lean opportunities on and off the shop floor.

The lapse in the collective judgment of companies in dealing with waste in information management typically creates at least twice as much waste in the office as on the shop floor. As pointed out in Chapter 1, this waste also negatively affects the company's ability to remain competitive through a lean transformation throughout the enterprise. This is why it is important that the company, as well as the value-stream team members, have or develop a working knowledge of lean principles to complement this workbook. There are many excellent books to educate the workforce, such as *Lean Thinking* (Womack and Jones, 1996), *Becoming Lean* (edited by Jeffrey Liker, 1997), and *Lean Lexicon* (edited by Chet Marchwinski and John Shook, 2003).

Determining Value from Waste in Administrative Activities

Two categories of actions are involved to design, order, and make a specific product or deliver a specific service. These are actions that:

1. Create value as perceived by the customer.

2. Create *no* value as perceived by the customer but are currently required to support the various needs of the business.

Most of the work processes that take place in the office are in the second group. These actions are required to support the existing business model, so the company cannot eliminate them until it reconsiders a new business model. When a company begins the path to become a lean enterprise it must challenge the entire business model. Otherwise, the actions in the second group will remain intact and the company may not be able to attain its business strategy.

This is why one of the first orders of business for the team members in understanding the office value stream is to be able to distinguish value from waste. Administrative wastes abound, and Table 3-1 lists some simple examples to stimulate the thought processes of team members. Learning to distinguish between value and waste begins with recognizing the many activities that are performed every day in a business for what they really are—waste that adds cost to the business, but no value to the customer. While most lean efforts focus on the first seven wastes shown in Table 3-1, we have added an eighth, *underutilized people*, to reflect waste created by not using a person's full mental, creative, and physical abilities. Some of the examples in the table may surprise you.

TEAM REMINDER

The activities employees engage in can actually include non-value-added tasks currently required or needed by a process or customer in the company's current business model. It is the job of the team to recognize the true nature of waste in business processes before designing and implementing new value streams supporting a lean enterprise.

Team Exercise: As a team orientation exercise, identify office waste and its root causes utilizing the five-why technique. Once team members have identified some examples of waste, they should ask the question "why" five times whenever they encounter a reason for the waste. Repeatedly asking the question "why" leads the team to identifying its root cause. This root cause exercise often leads to many surprises, questions, and discussions.

Table 3-1. Eight Wastes That Add Costs to the Business but No Value to the Customer

Waste Category	Office Examples
1. Overproducing Producing more, sooner, or faster than is required by the next process	Printing paperwork out before it is really needed, purchasing items before they are needed, processing paperwork before the next person is ready for it
2. Inventory Any form of batch processing	Filled in-boxes (electronic and paper), office supplies, sales literature, batch processing transactions and reports
3. Waiting	System downtime, system response time, approvals from others, information from customers
4. Extra Processing	Re-entering data, extra copies, unnecesary or excessive reports, transactions, cost accounting, expediting, labor reporting, budget processes, travel expense reporting, month-end closing activities
5. Correction Any form of defects	Order entry errors, design errors and engineering change orders, invoice errors, employee turnover
6. Excess Motion Movement of people	Walking to/from copier, central filing, fax machine, other offices
7. Transportation Movement of paperwork	Excessive email attachments, multiple hand-offs, multiple approvals
8. Underutilized People People's abilities, not their time	Limited employee authority and responsibility for basic tasks, management command and control, inadequate business tools available

When companies do address waste in the office environment, the initial reaction of many is to address all forms of waste and redesign any and all the business processes at once. This scattershot approach is time and resource consuming, and generally ineffective in its application. A more effective approach is to do a value stream map at the site level, revealing the big picture first, thus helping the company focus resources on the critical areas of waste that require immediate attention for the enterprise to remain competitive.

For most companies, the cost, service, and quality of many office activities are hidden from the customer or have little to do with directly servicing the customer. This "distance" from the customer has created support functions with little appreciation of, or measurement of, the waste generated in their work. While the shop floor has performance metrics that highlight and stimulate a response to problems (and waste), the office is typically void of such diligence. Similar metrics are required in the office to support maximizing the work value and minimizing the waste. (We will discuss distinctive office metrics in Chapter 5.)

Now the team is ready to follow the case study of ABC Design Company. In the next chapter, we provide an overview of how the company used value stream mapping as a tool and lean as a strategy to improve its competitive position for the whole organization. We will also introduce the first of many value stream maps of ABC Design.

CHAPTER 4

ABC Design's Lean Transformation in the Production Area

ABC Design Company is in the business of designing and fabricating high-end custom office layouts and furniture. They have struggled to remain competitive in recent years, mainly due to a long lead time for their products. The market has come to expect an eight-week lead time, while ABC Design is currently at 12 to14 weeks. As a result, sales have declined by 20 percent during the past two years. In an attempt to reduce lead time and become more competitive, ABC Design Company looked to lean concepts for answers. Its emphasis on customer requirements and lead time reduction seemed to fit the company's needs.

ABC Design decided to apply lean concepts in the production area. "After all, isn't lean a manufacturing concept?" the owner said. The results after one year were impressive: a 40 percent productivity improvement and a seven-day reduction in production lead time from 12 days to 5 days. The production area now has its new value stream represented on the current state map (Figure 4-1).

Let's briefly review ABC's new production system moving from customer information, to information flow, to material flow and finally, supplier information.

Customer Information

The customer icon is in the top right corner of Figure 4-1.

- ABC's customer base is represented by about 100 contractors ordering a total of 250 jobs per year, or about one a day.

- The customers have a lead time requirement of eight weeks.

- Jobs are shipped daily by truck, as shown on the right side of the map.

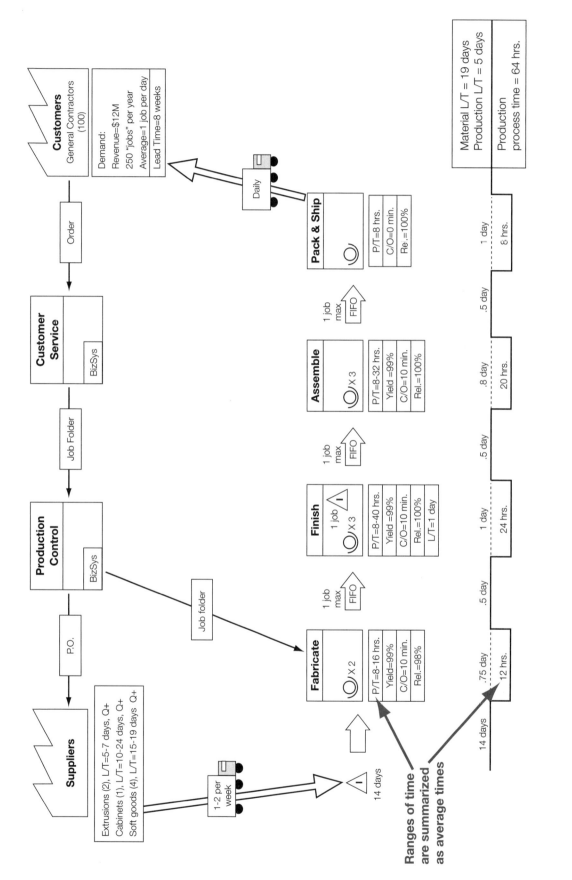

Figure 4-1. ABC Design Current State Map of Value Stream for the Production Area

Information Flow

Information moves from right to left on the top half of the map.

- Orders are sent from the contractors to customer service, with information then relayed to production control. (Note: this is a simplistic view of the information flow, as we shall see later!)

- Production control then triggers suppliers to send in material via purchase orders.

- Production control also triggers jobs to begin within production via job folders released in the fabrication area.

- Production triggers within the material flow are created through FIFO (first-in, first-out) lanes between the work areas, with a maximum of one job (i.e., a range of zero to one job) allowed between each process.

The FIFO lanes are structured to contain a fixed maximum amount of work in progress between two tasks, and minimize overproduction on the shop floor. If one of the processes completes its portion of a job and fills the FIFO lane, it can't begin more work until the downstream customer process pulls the work out of the FIFO lane. To make this system work effectively, workers are cross-trained to support both the upstream and downstream work. They can then flex upstream and downstream to keep the work moving according to what the FIFO lane rules dictate. In this manner, the company controls the flow of materials between processes.

Material Flow

Material flows from left to right on the bottom half of the map.

- There are four production process boxes: fabricate, finish, assemble, and pack and ship, which is how each job progresses through the shop.

- Each of the four process boxes have a process data box underneath them with performance related information such as yield, changeover time (C/O), equipment reliability (Rel.), process time on a per job basis (P/T), and in the data box under finish, lead time (L/T) to account for finish drying times.

- The bottom of the map shows a staggered timeline that compares the processing time for a job to the production lead time of the job on the floor. The dashed lines can represent the lead time impact of multiple operators on a job.

Supplier Information

- Material is brought into the plant by truck from external suppliers as depicted on the left side of the map, with the suppliers listed in the top left corner. The raw material inventory is depicted as a triangle under the truck.

- Supplier performance information is shown in the data box below the supplier icon, including the number of suppliers for that particular component or material—that is, extrusions (2), typical lead time (L/T), and a general statement of supplier quality performance (i.e., Q+, representing excellent quality).

Team Note: When the team reviews the supply base, they should focus on the critical, high value items or materials. They should not list *all* of the suppliers for all of the materials consumed in the business but instead focus on the critical few.

Once ABC Design established a lean production system, however, it continued to lose orders due to its uncompetitive lead time: its lead time was still 10 to 12 weeks. To find a remedy ABC Design once again turned to value stream mapping, but this time they looked at their preproduction processes. Chapter 6 outlines this process step-by-step, but first the team must review the steps to complete a current state map, including how to select the process metrics for an office environment.

CHAPTER 5

Assessing the Office Current State

As discussed earlier, the current state map represents the documentation of how a company is currently doing business and is the basis for designing a future state and initiating true Value Stream Management. To begin developing the current state map, the team needs to understand not only the physical steps of drawing the map, but what metrics to select to measure the effectiveness of the enterprise in terms of cost, service, and quality. For the purposes of this workbook, we chose six steps to help the team in both of these areas. In this chapter, we will spend most of the time discussing process metrics. In Chapter 6, we will apply all six steps to ABC Design's effort at creating a site-level current state map. As the mapping team moves forward, these steps should be used as a guideline to create a current state map.

Suggested Steps to Complete a Current State Map

1. Document customer information and need.

2. Identify main processes (in order).

3. Select process metrics.

4. Perform value stream walk-through and fill in data boxes, including inventory and resident technology.

5. Establish how each process prioritizes work.

6. Calculate system summary metrics, such as lead time versus process time, first-pass yield, cost, and/or other value stream summary measures.

Step 1: Document Customer Information and Need

The team should use the outside resource icon to represent the customer or customers (see Figure 5-1). A data box should be added below defining the customer needs or requirements (e.g., demand, lead time).

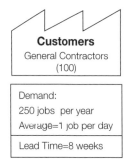

Customers
General Contractors
(100)

Demand:
250 jobs per year
Average=1 job per day

Lead Time=8 weeks

Figure 5-1. Displaying Customer Need

Step 2: Identify Main Processes (in Order)

It is important that *processes* be identified in the process box—not departments or functions. The focus is on the activities required to process information, not titles or names of people. Sometimes, a mapping team insists on noting the department currently performing the task. They can note this in a process box, if necessary (see Figure 5-2). The team usually completes this step in the classroom or conference room and makes any necessary changes as they walk the process (Step 4).

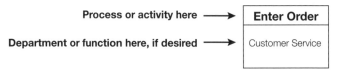

Process or activity here ⟶ | **Enter Order**

Department or function here, if desired ⟶ | Customer Service

Figure 5-2. Displaying Department or Function in a Process Box

Step 3: Selecting Process Metrics

Selecting metrics for current state maps can be troublesome since most administrative processes have no standard performance metrics reflecting cost, service, and quality within the value stream. The team can apply many of the shop floor metrics from *Learning to See* in developing a map reflecting the entire enterprise. In addition, there are distinctive metrics that lend themselves well to the office environment.

The process metrics that follow are a good starting point for the team. They may find several of these metrics are unique to the organization or they might select other metrics to support the visualization of the process and inherent problems in the value stream. Of course, not all metrics apply to every process.

Process Metrics

1. Time: process time, lead time, and value-added time.

2. Changeover time.

3. Typical batch sizes or practices.

4. Demand rate.

5. Percent complete and accurate.

6. Reliability.

7. Number of people.

8. Inventory.

9. Information technology used.

10. Available time.

Mapping Note. We are discussing these ten metrics to suggest possible ways to measure a company's process. Don't use all of them! Select a few that makes sense and get started with a map to see what you learn. *Always* include process time and lead time.

Time

There are several definitions of process, lead, and value-added time. We offer definitions the team can use to be consistent while determining the company's value stream design (see Figure 5-3).

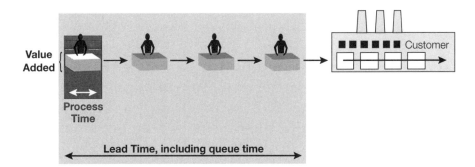

Figure 5-3. Process Time, Lead Time, and Value-Added Time

Process Time (P/T). This is the actual time it takes to complete a process or activity. The team can usually quantify process time by observation. For example, it takes five minutes to enter an order from beginning to end, uninterrupted. Process times may vary for a variety of reasons (e.g., worker capability, customer type, order type, etc.). When this happens, the team needs to determine whether these variations represent different service families, or if some other explanation exists. The data could then be displayed in a range (e.g., 5 to 10 minutes per order) with a note as to why the variation occurs.

Lead Time (L/T). This is the elapsed time associated with completing an activity. It is measured from the time it enters the in-box to the time it leaves a desk complete (normally to the next in-box). Lead time is generally greater than process time as work can sit in a queue, either waiting for someone to begin the process, or waiting for someone to complete it due to interruptions. For example, it may take just five minutes to enter an order (i.e., process time). However, questions might arise and the person puts the order aside for a period of time. Therefore, the five-minute order entry task may actually take two hours to complete (i.e., lead time) while the order is in queue waiting for answers. The team can also note reasons for excessive lead time such as order errors or multiple interruptions.

Value-Added Time. Typically, this is the portion of process time that employees actually spend on value-added activities. The team does not usually capture value-added time during site level or cross-functional level mapping, but at the process level.

> *Lean Note:* If a worker practices true one-piece flow, or process one, move one without interruption, then process time equals lead time. An example of this is to process an order and hand it to the next person in the value stream, who then immediately begins to process the information.

Changeover Time

Changeover time is the time it takes to change from one activity to another. For example, let's say that the same printer is used to print invoices and statements. If it takes 10 minutes to go to the printer, change the paper from statements to invoices, align the paper and print out an invoice, a changeover time of 10 minutes exists. Another example of changeover time might be associated with retrieving documentation from a central file before beginning to work.

A subtle example of changeover can be changing from one computer screen to another. At one company, it took six distinct steps to move from an order entry screen to an inventory screen. Altogether, the changeover time was one minute, including system response time. While this does not sound significant, this activity occurred 50 times a day!

Another example is the change from one task to another, which is common in an office environment. People will often stop an activity, put it aside and start another activity, then return to the first activity later on, requiring several minutes to re-acclimate themselves to the work. This can occur for many reasons, particularly when the person requires additional information or direction, or has general work interruptions. This form of mental changeover is disruptive and negatively impacts a person's productivity. While difficult to measure, the team might wish to discuss how frequently a person has to put aside work and the time it takes for the person to refocus his or her thoughts on the work when it is resumed. Changeover time typically creates a need to batch work and extends the lead time of a value stream.

Typical Batch Sizes or Practices

Typical batch sizes or batching practices represent how much or how often work is performed. In many administrative functions, a certain routine is established. For example, the accounting function in a small manufacturing company might follow this routine:

- Mondays: Invoices.

- Tuesdays: Payables.

- Wednesdays: General Ledger.

- Thursdays: Payroll.

- Fridays: Reports.

In this example, every activity is being performed once per week, creating a batch size of one week. With paperwork (e.g., invoices) waiting in a batch as long as one week, the lead time could be as high as one week. So, this batch size can be related to lead time, and in cases such as this, it may make sense to use this in place of the traditional lead time.

Demand Rate

Demand rate represents the volume of transactions seen at each process over a specified period, such as orders per day, line items per order, etc. This is a key attribute, as it explicitly states a customer requirement. The team uses this metric to design a system capable of responding to customer requirements.

If applicable, the team should also note the range of demand along with a note explaining the variation. As an example, one company we worked with completed 80 percent of the invoicing in the last week of each month.

The demand rate unit of measure will change based on the nature of the activity. For example, the number of orders received per day may be an appropriate measure of demand on an order processing activity in one organization. In other companies, a more appropriate measure will be the number of line items. The number of shipped orders per day may be an appropriate measure of demand on an invoicing process, since the number of line items on an order may be irrelevant to the invoicing process. However, for a pick and pack process, the number of line items is usually the more appropriate metric.

Percent Complete and Accurate

Percent complete and accurate (% C&A) is a process quality metric used to describe how often an activity receives information that is complete and accurate from the perspective of the recipient. Paperwork or other transactions might not contain necessary information, or might be confusing or illegible. The % C&A attribute is one way to quantify the inability of the process to meet the internal customer requirements within the value stream, which typically results in extending both the process time and lead time to support the value stream.

For instance, if an order is faxed to customer service, they might review the order for legibility, ship-to, etc. The percentage of orders customer service enters without a problem is the % C&A. Extending this example, if engineering then reviews the entered order it might find some technical information missing from the order. In this case, engineering might have a different % C&A baseline, as it has a different perspective on an order requirement.

Table 5-1 provides other suggested quality measures for various nonproduction processes and includes several examples of rework or revisions in the office.

Reliability

Reliability is the percentage of time that a piece of equipment (usually a computer) is available when needed. Just as in production, office processes rely on equipment to perform necessary business functions. However, few companies actually measure the reliability of this equipment. Reliability can be affected by such issues as true IT system downtime, which can include access to departmental software, such as shipping or purchase order programs. It can also include poorly designed software or operator error that causes the

Table 5-1. Possible Quality Measures by Nonproduction Business Process

Business Process	Possible Quality Measures
Invoicing	• Number of adjustments, dollar amount of adjustments, or adjustments as a percentage of total sales revenue
Engineering Design	• Number of engineering changes required after release of the design to production
Scheduling	• Number of rush or expedited orders • Number of late shipments
Purchasing	• Number of purchased part shortages • Number or percentage of incorrect parts or materials ordered • Number of rush or expedited orders
Quoting and Estimating	• "Hit Rate"—The percentage of quotes that become actual orders
Accounts Receivable	• Days outstanding, bad debt as a percentage of sales
Inventory Control	• Cycle count accuracy

software to easily crash, causing the need for rework. Or there may be insufficient software licenses for everyone who depends on the IT system to complete their work. A fourth example is the software slowing down at different times of the day or week, causing longer response times to inquiries. Poor reliability can create long lead times, process times, and possible quality problems within a value stream.

Number of People

The number of people metric can represent one of two situations. The first situation is simply the number of people trained to do or responsible for doing the work. For instance, there could be four people capable of entering orders, even though only one person physically enters them at any point in time. This representation shows how widespread the task knowledge is, identifying issues of cross-training, or the lack thereof. A good question to ask is: "Is this the only person who knows how to perform this activity?" Cross-training is often lacking in administrative processes since many activities can be put on hold until the one person who knows how to perform the activity can get to it.

The second way to use the number of people metric is to represent the number of full-time equivalents (sometimes referred to as FTEs) needed to regularly perform each business process. When used with process time, the number of people can be compared with the demand rate to verify the capacity of each business process. For example, if a transaction takes 30 minutes to complete at a certain step and the value stream has a demand of

20 transactions a day, then a capacity of 600 minutes a day is necessary to support the value stream at that step.

Estimating the number of people and the percentage of time that they typically spend on a specific task can be difficult in an office environment. Office personnel often perform multiple tasks and are unaware of how they are spending their time. Normally, their best guess is sufficient for our purposes here. For example, five people might estimate that they spend approximately 20 percent of their time performing a specific process. In this case, you can depict the percent with a simple formula (see Figure 5-4). In this example, we can easily determine that there is one full-time equivalent person currently performing this task.

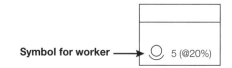

Figure 5-4. Icon Indicating Percent of Time to Perform a Specific Process

Mapping Tip. For various reasons it may be difficult to overcome people's reluctance to estimate the percentage of time they spend on a task. At times, it may be necessary for the team to collect this information over time—say one week—in order to firm up the estimate. Then they can revise the data on the current state map, if necessary. In this way, the team can easily overcome a difficult obstacle to the mapping process while getting the necessary information.

Inventory

Inventory can take many forms in administrative processes and represents queues of information and symptoms of a lack of flow. Inventory typically resides as paperwork or electronic files. The unit of measure can vary based on the nature of the business process. Examples include:

- Orders queued at the fax machine.
- Various forms in people's in-boxes.
- Work stored in e-mails (e.g., messages, requests for information, files).
- Design projects in queue or underway.
- Line items awaiting purchasing to process, etc.

Figure 5-5 depicts piles of paperwork or electronic queues of information. Inventory is normally associated with batch processing and long lead times.

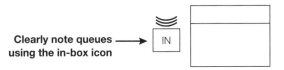

Figure 5-5. Icon Indicating Inventory in the Office

Team Exercise: Compare observed inventory against the demand rate for a process in order to estimate a lead time. For example, if a company receives on average 50 orders per day, and there are 25 orders that have yet to be entered, then it is safe to say there are 0.5 days of orders in queue (25 orders divided by 50 orders per day = 0.5 days). As a cross-check, compare the computed lead time to the observed lead time and batching practices, if they exist. If, for example, customer service stops by the fax machine twice a day you would expect a half a day's worth of orders to accumulate. If the numbers compare favorably, then the team's data is in the neighborhood.

Information Technology Used

Information technology used describes the software tools used to assist the processing of the information at each process box. While this is not a true "metric," it is an important attribute we include in describing the value stream. The team records this in a lower corner of the process box (see Figure 5-6). There may be several technologies used within a process box, and several others used in different process boxes. This apparent lack of integration can be a root cause for long lead times, lack of flow, extra processing, and quality related problems.

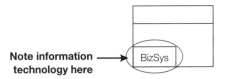

Figure 5-6. Icon Indicating Information Technology Used to Assist the Processing of Information

Available Time

Available time is the amount of time that a company is open for business and is able to perform a particular process or processes, or the effective working time over the course of a day. For example, let's say that the customer service department is only staffed on one shift, and the shift runs from 8:00 A.M. to 4:30 P.M. The total shift time is 510 minutes. However, customer service personnel take 30 minutes for lunch and get two 10-minute breaks each day. Therefore, the available time is really 460 minutes (510 – 30 –10 – 10 = 460 minutes).

Available time may be important to note when the value stream supports multiple transactional information processes (e.g., invoices, orders, journal entries). It will help determine the necessary capacity to a support the demand with a structured pace of work. If the individual process steps operate with different available times, the team should note the times in the process data boxes.

Sometimes an entire group of processes operates under the same circumstances. For example, the entire office operates on the same schedule. Then it may simply be desirable to record this fact in a box somewhere on the current state map; for example:

$$\text{Available time for all processes} = \text{460 minutes per shift, one shift operation throughout}$$

However, sometimes office personnel are not available as much as it might seem. For example, some office personnel travel a great deal. The team should consider this in the available time estimate and calculation. For example, a buyer may spend an average of 20 percent of his or her time visiting existing or potential suppliers. Therefore, instead of 460 minutes we might note 368 minutes (80% of 460 minutes) with a note regarding the travel. Another example is the time people spend in communication meetings, training, etc. that have nothing to do with directly supporting the work in a value stream.

Keys to Selecting Process Metrics

The purpose of value stream metrics is to help visualize a process and identify process issues. The metrics we've discussed are helpful in most cases, but aren't intended to represent every situation. There may be specific issues to make visual in a particular company's value streams that will require some creative metrics or icons to "tell the story." Here are some keys to remember when selecting metrics.

- The information the team collects while documenting the current state map quantifies the cost, service, and quality performance of the various elements of the value stream.

- In many cases, the team uses the collected documentation to highlight areas of value, waste, and impediments to flow.

- The team can make the list of metrics as flexible as they wish, considering other metrics that are relevant to a particular business process. Use metrics that help the team to see what is truly happening in the enterprise. Be creative!

- In many cases, the first value stream map the team creates will contain a lot of estimated data since there is very little process performance data collected in most offices. However, there is a message here: If the team sees the value in these metrics, they should consider establishing simple, quick ways of collecting this data on an ongoing basis to help manage the value stream within the context of a lean enterprise.

Step 4: Perform Value Stream Walk-Through

This step is the main event for creating the current state map. It consumes most of the day as the team uses this opportunity to understand how work is created, progresses, and is organized. The team should make every effort to "walk" through this value stream from beginning to end, immersing themselves in the process. To complete this step, the team observes each of the main process steps identified in Step 2 and collects the agreed-upon data at each step. The team should feel free to ask questions necessary to identify issues and understand the work as it progresses and creates value.

Step 5: Establish How Each Process Prioritizes Work

The prioritization of work represents the information flow of a value stream in an office process. While the information flow is more structured and apparent on the shop floor (via specific schedules or instructions), work prioritization is typically informal in most office activities. For instance, some people might arrange their work by due date, while others might arrange their work by the size of the order. Different priorities generally cause longer and inconsistent lead times. The team can document the scheduling activity of each process box by noting how the people in the process prioritize the in-box of work (see Figure 5-7).

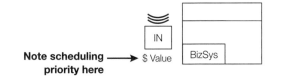

Figure 5-7. Icon for Scheduling the Activity of Each Process Box

To document how employees prioritize their work within the value stream, the team should ask each person how they manage their work as well as observe how they perform it during the team's walk-through. The answers might be quite interesting! Remember, this is very useful information for challenging how people should prioritize their work in an improved value stream.

Step 6: Calculate System Summary Metrics

When the team has completed the walk-through, they assess the value stream performance from a systems perspective. The lead time and process times can be represented on a time line at the bottom of the map, and each summarized for the entire value stream. Although it's possible to document ranges of time in process data boxes, it's less confusing to average this range in the time line. Quality and cost metrics that the team has selected can also be summarized for the value stream. We will see how this is done for ABC Design in Chapter 6. The team should plan to use some or all of these metrics on a permanent basis to gauge the effectiveness and efficiency of the work within the future state designs. However, the team should take care not to create a massive data collection system to support the effort. Instead, keep it simple and visual. We'll show you how to do this in Chapter 6 when we design the current state map for ABC Design.

The mapping tips in the following box sum up the discussion for Steps 3 through 6 in this chapter. The team can use these as a quick reference during mapping activities.

Tips for Mapping the Current State

- *Identify the basic process boxes before performing the actual walk-through.* This helps the team agree on the level of detail they will use throughout the mapping. Included here is identifying the customers and suppliers (internal and/or external) to the identified value stream. This adequately sets boundaries for the mapping exercise by establishing the starting and ending points of the map. The team can add or subtract process boxes as necessary during the actual walk-through.

- *Identify the metrics that the team will collect for each process box.* At this point the team should agree on a definition for each metric. Doing this before the actual walk-through minimizes confusion and greatly speeds up the mapping process.

- *Add other information (via visual icons or metrics) as you observe the process steps in motion.* Be flexible, as there is no perfect current state map!

- *Guard against making the map too unwieldy; start simply, and add boxes as necessary.* For example, if a series of activities is completed in a relatively short period (i.e., as compared to the overall expected lead time and the demand rate), use one process box to represent the entire group of activities.

- *Estimate the performance of the current state the first time through to get a quick picture of the value stream as it exists.* Most office processes have little true performance data, and it could take weeks or months to generate accurate data. Save the time and get estimates from the people who perform these tasks.

- *Walk the value stream to gather the performance data associated with creating the value.* Mapping should not take place entirely in a meeting or conference room. Team members gain a higher level of knowledge as they personally witness each activity. Don't count on seeing all activities performed in minute detail: this is a "high level" perspective. Observe the major tasks involved in the value stream such as an actual order or an invoice being generated. Ask to see examples of the types of major problems that arise.

- *Ask questions regarding activities and issues you see to understand potential barriers in designing future states.* For example, there may be batching of paperwork at particular steps that may cause delays or create quality problems in subsequent steps. Why is work performed this way? Will this affect how the team thinks about the future state designs?

- *Map the whole value stream as a team.* If possible, avoid different people mapping different segments of the value stream. Understanding and seeing only a portion of the value stream creates a disconnected picture of the complete organization.

- *Assign team members specific tasks to perform in the mapping process.* This ensures that the mapping activities will be completed and the members stay engaged in the process. Ask one member to be the data recorder, making certain that the team fills out all metrics. Another member can be a scribe, recording any issues or

Continued on next page

ideas that are sure to arise during the walk-through. Still another member can be a timekeeper, measuring actual process times wherever possible, and keeping the team on track.

- *Always draw by hand and in pencil.* Drawing by hand creates minimal delay during the walk-through. In addition, it might be difficult to map and discuss the process performance at the same time, so discuss the map at each process step to identify additional information that you need and make changes before moving on. That's why we always use pencils (and erasers)!

CHAPTER 6

Designing the Current State Map for ABC Design

In this chapter, we apply the six-step process to complete a site-level current state map for ABC Design. As discussed in Chapter 4, ABC Design began its lean journey by mapping the shop floor value streams but soon realized that it needed to expand its lean effort throughout the organization. As a result, it assembled a cross-functional mapping team representing sales, customer service, engineering, materials management, production, and accounting. Once ABC put together a team, other employees participated as needed to complete the mapping of the office value streams.

In scoping the site-level value stream, the team examined the company's two main product lines and agreed that the process steps, particularly in the non-production areas, were unaffected by which product the customer purchased. The real variation was job specific, and affected the process times of the various functions, rather than the steps themselves. "We are a job shop," team members often commented. Therefore, the team agreed that there was really only one overall family for understanding the enterprise at the site level. Once this was established, the team could begin following the methodology and steps involved in creating a current state map.

To illustrate how the ABC team identified and documented the various processes, we will be using the same set of value stream mapping symbols and icons used in Figure 4-1 and steps outlined in Chapter 5. *Note:* Figures marked 6-1A and 6-1B are to be read side by side.

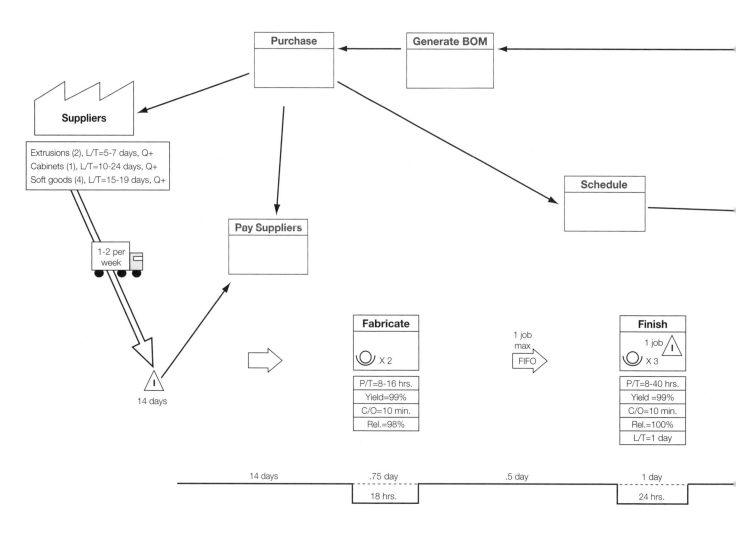

Figure 6-1A. Current State Map Identifying Eight Main Processes

Step 1. Documenting Customer Information and Need

The mapping in value stream design always begins with identifying the customer requirements, including the output of the work that has value as perceived by the customer, keeping in mind that the customer may be internal or external. ABC Design documented its customer requirements during the process of creating its current state map of the production system (see Figure 4-1), so the team repeated this step for its site-level map.

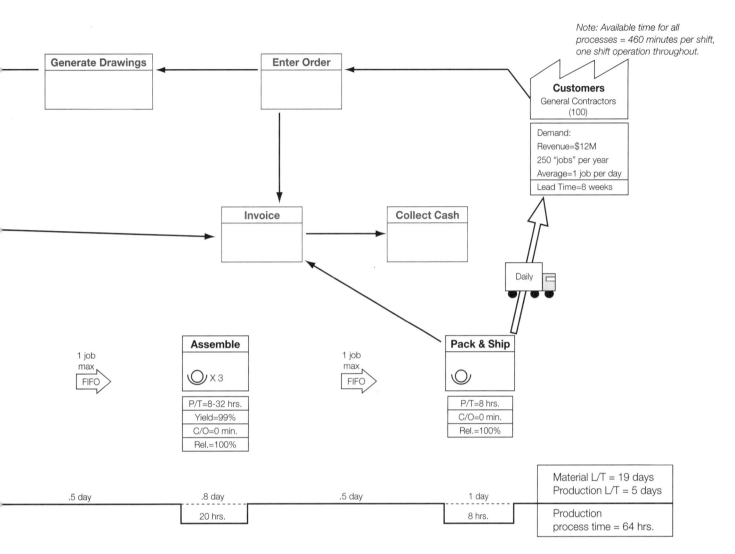

Figure 6-1B. Current State Map Identifying Eight Main Processes (*continued*)

Step 2. Identifying Main Processes (in Order)

The mapping team identified eight main processes in the company's office activities and created a process box for each one (see Figure 6-1A and B). Each of the process steps is discussed in Steps 3 and 4.

For ABC Design, each process operated on a single shift. The available time for each shift was 460 minutes. The company used overtime when necessary.

Steps 3 and 4. Selecting Process Metrics and Filling in the Data Boxes

The team selected metrics for each of ABC's process boxes and collected data, including paperwork inventory and resident technology, by walking the process from beginning to end. Following are ABC Design's process metrics and data collections for each of the eight main process boxes. *Note:* All lead times are shown in business days (five days/week), not calendar days (seven days/week).

> *Mapping Tip:* If your company relies on outside services to perform particular business functions (e.g. payroll, design) you can use the outside resource icon to identify this if these activities are within the scope of the mapping effort.

1. *Enter order.* There are two people responsible for completing the review and entry of orders. If they find a problem while reviewing the paperwork, they generate and return a discrepancy form to the sales representative for correction.

   - Process time for one person to complete and review one order, taking into account generating the occasional discrepancy form, ranges from 30 minutes to 1 hour.

   - Lead time for enter order ranges from one to seven days. The primary reason for the large range is that it takes time to resolve problems identified with an order.

   - Quality of the information (% C&A) provided by the sales representatives is estimated to be 60 percent: 60 percent of all orders are submitted with complete and accurate information, 40 percent have some associated problems such as missing color, incorrect fabric called out, or missing dimension.

   - Orders are entered into the BizSys system at an average of one per day which also alerts the Invoice task to the job.

   - The availability or reliability of the BizSys system has been estimated at 90 percent.

   - A job folder is generated with a copy of the order, as well as the information received from the sales representative, which is provided to the people who generate the drawings.

   - Currently three jobs have discrepancy forms and are waiting resolution.

   We now add the enter order process information to the map, represented in Figure 6-2B. (There are no changes to Figure 6-2A at this time.)

2. *Generate drawings.* Using information from the plans and the order, computer-aided drawings (CAD) for each job are generated. There are two CAD operators.

- Process time ranges from 1 to 40 hours per job, depending on the size and complexity of the job.
- Lead time through the drawing process ranges from 1 to 10 days.
- Engineers use a drawing system called ACAD. Availability or reliability of the ACAD software and hardware is 85 percent.
- The quality of the drawing process is estimated to be 95 percent. Approximately 5 percent of all drawings generated have some problem with them (e.g., incorrect call-outs).
- Once the drawings are complete, they are added to the job folder and passed on to the people who generate the bill-of-material for each job. A copy is also sent to the customer for approval. Typical customer approval lead time is 15 business days (three weeks).

3. *Generate BOM (bill-of-material).* Four people perform a manual review of the job folder to develop a list of materials that need to be purchased and manufactured.

- Process time to generate a bill-of-material ranges from 8 to 40 hours per job.
- Lead time to generate the bill-of-material is one to two days.
- Quality of the BOM process is 80 percent. That is, 20 percent of all BOMs have missing or incorrect information. Typically, however, these problems are not discovered until the assembly process. Therefore, the team adds it to the Assemble data box.
- One copy of the BOM is provided to purchasing and another placed in the job folder for the scheduler.

We now add the information from the generate drawings and generate BOM processes to Figure 6-3A.

4. *Purchase.* Two buyers take the order information and BOM to identify all items that must be purchased. The buyers contact existing suppliers, or identify new sources if necessary. Purchase orders are generated for each job that suppliers confirm with an expected ship date.

- Process time ranges from 4 to 12 hours per job.
- All purchase orders are placed for a job within a lead time of one day.
- The buyers enter purchase orders on the BizSys system. The availability or reliability of the BizSys system is 90 percent.
- The buyers process approximately 20 line items per job per day.

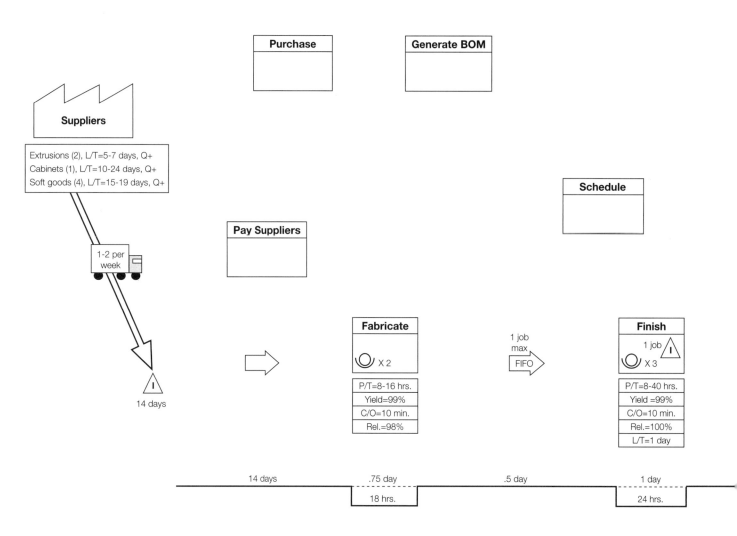

Figure 6-2A. Enter Order Process Information Added (No Changes)

5. *Schedule.* The person responsible for scheduling receives the job folder and waits for receipt of all purchased items before releasing it to fabrication.

• The production coordinator uses a spreadsheet to assist in the scheduling process.

• The process time for scheduling is two hours per job.

We now add the information from the Purchase and Schedule processes to Figure 6-4A.

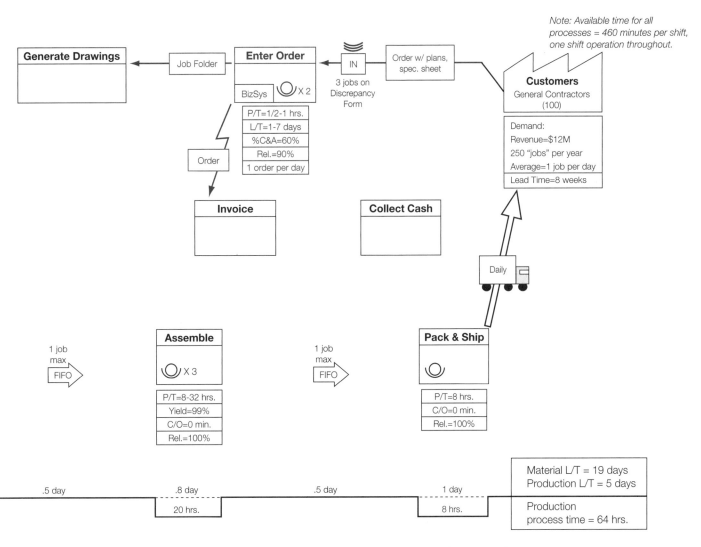

Figure 6-2B. Enter Order Process Information Added (*continued*)

6. *Invoice.* An invoice is generated for each job upon shipment to the customer.

- One person is assigned this task, and uses the BizSys system to process the information.
- Process time is 10 minutes.
- Lead time is one day once the shipping department has submitted the bill of lading (BOL).
- On average, one invoice per day is processed using BizSys.
- In the past year, ABC Design made numerous invoice adjustments representing 1.6 percent of total sales revenue, or $200,000. Changes were usually initiated because of a customer disputing a charge on the invoice.

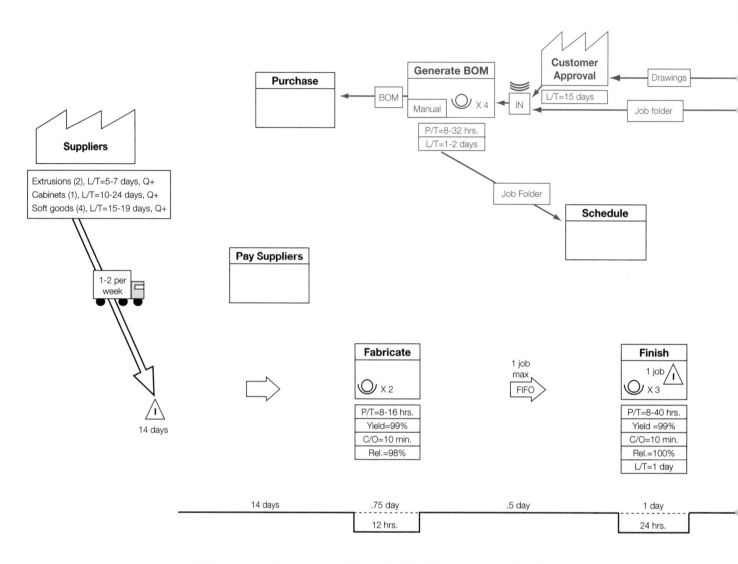

Figure 6-3A. Generate Drawings and Generate BOM Process Information Added

7. *Collect cash.* One person receives and applies the checks from the customers.

- The process time is 0 to 60 minutes per invoice.
- The invoices and checks for accounts receivable are supported by the BizSys system.
- Currently, total accounts receivable is $2,000,000 or approximately 45 business days of outstanding invoices, which represents the lead time.

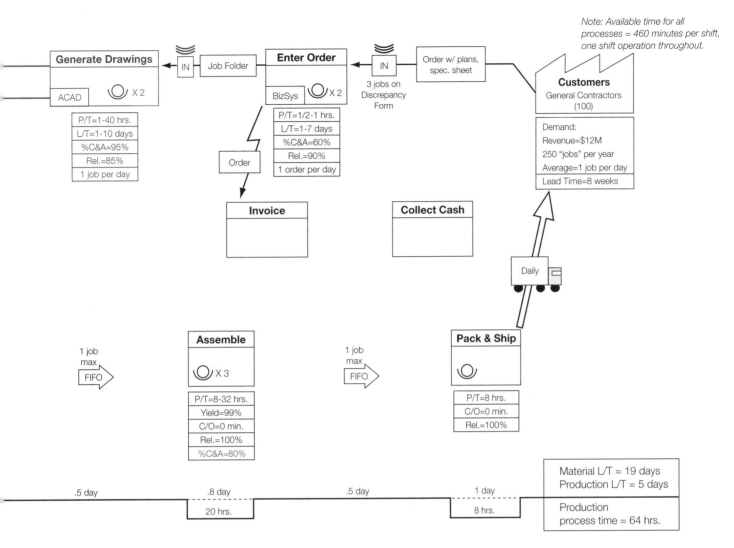

Figure 6-3B. Generate Drawings and Generate BOM Process Information Added (*continued*)

8. *Pay suppliers.* This activity includes the traditional three-way match of purchase order, supplier invoice, and a receiving document. One person is assigned this responsibility and uses BizSys to support the activity.

- Currently, total accounts payable is $100,000 or about 15 business days of outstanding supplier invoices, representing the lead time.

- The process time is 15 minutes per invoice.

We now add the information from the Invoice, Collect Cash, and Pay Suppliers processes to Figures 6-5A and 6-5B.

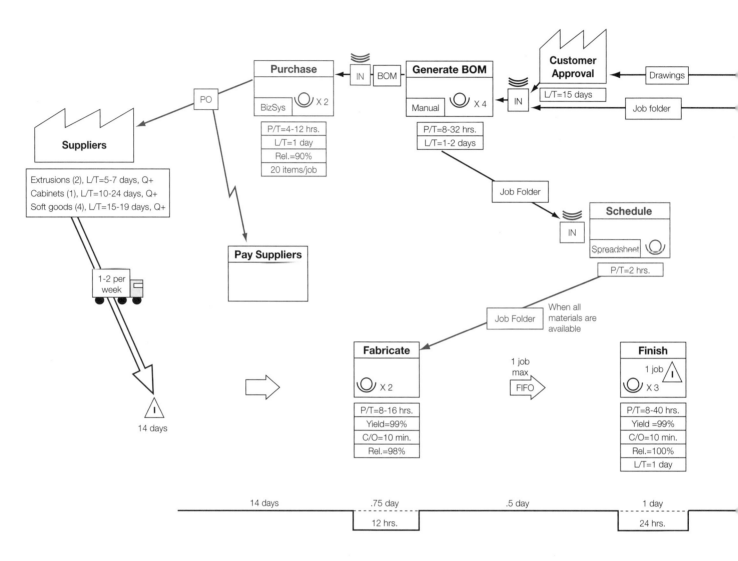

Figure 6-4A. Purchase and Schedule Process Information Added

Step 5. Establishing How Each Process Prioritizes Work

During the walk-through of the enterprise, ABC's mapping team asked workers how they prioritized their activities. Workers provided various responses but, in general, work was prioritized on a first-in-first-out basis, much the same way shop floor workers do in shop floor production flow. However, the priorities were different in for the Generate Drawings activity: here, the department manager said that he typically prioritizes by largest order (i.e., in terms of potential revenue to the company) first, unless otherwise directed by the owner. The team noted this on the current state map underneath the in-box for Generate Drawings.

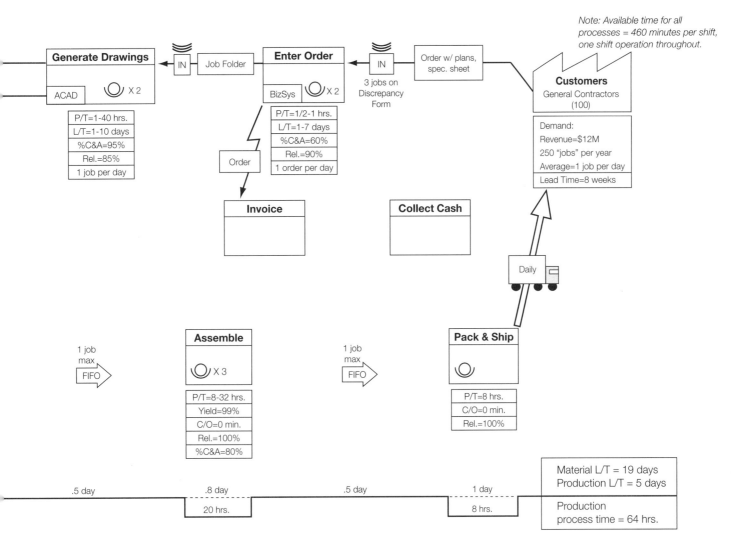

Figure 6-4B. Purchase and Schedule Process Information Added (*continued*)

Step 6. Calculating System Summary Metrics

Three summary metrics will be calculated: order-to-cash time, order lead time, and first-pass yield.

Order-to-Cash Time. As with shop floor mapping, the team quantifies an overall production lead time. However, in the case of office value stream mapping, the team must also quantify an *order-to-cash* lead time. The order-to-cash metric combines material lead time, preproduction time to process the order, as well as the postproduction time to invoice and collect money due.

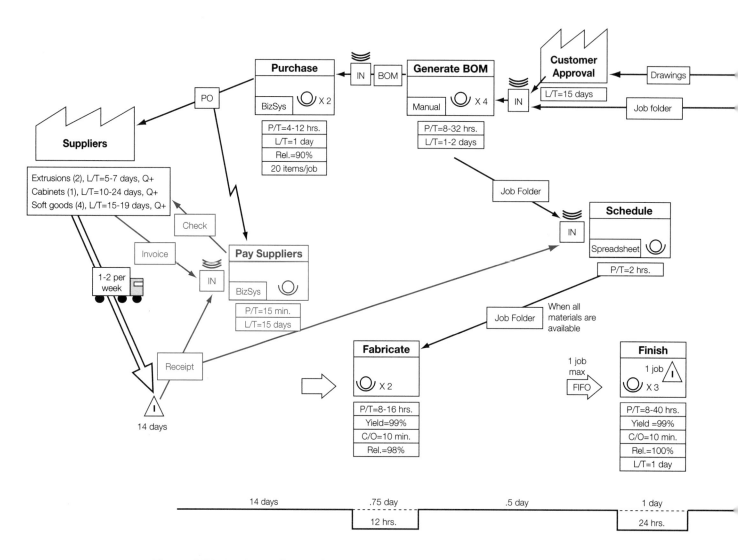

Figure 6-5A. Invoice, Collect Cash, and Pay Suppliers Process Information Added

The team quantified the preproduction lead time at 44 days: 27 business days to process an order upon receipt from the sales representative and/or customer plus an average (or mid-point) of 17 business days to receive the longest lead time materials from the suppliers. The material lead time through production and pack and ship is 5 days (rounded from 5.05 days). The postproduction lead time (i.e., the time to send the invoice and collect the cash) is 46 days. Therefore, the average total order-to-cash lead time is 95 days. This information is depicted on the current state map by using two time lines; one for preproduction at the top of the map (i.e., information management) and one for production at the bottom of the map (i.e., material flow), along with a summary box. To keep the visualization simple, there

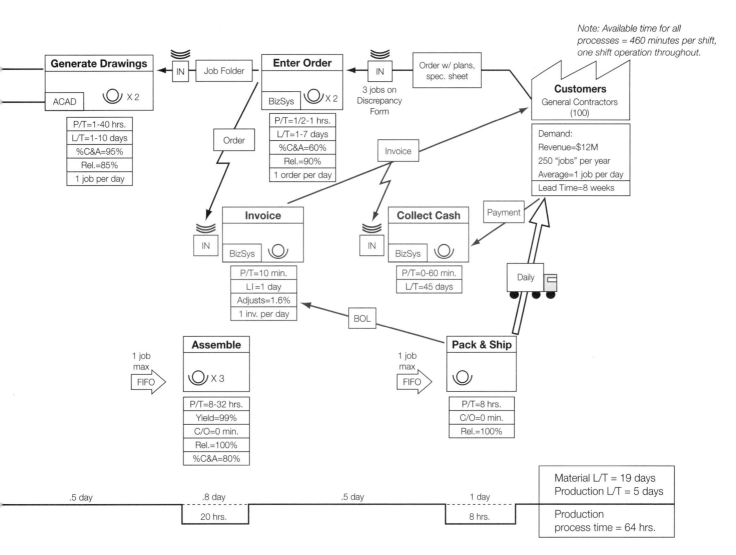

Figure 6-5B. Invoice, Collect Cash, and Pay Suppliers Process Information Added (*continued*)

is no third timeline for the postproduction activities (although you might want to add one).

Order Lead Time. The team also determined the overall time to process an order, depicted on the current state map, as the preproduction process time, as well as the production process time separately using the two time lines described in the previous section, along with a summary box. The current state order lead time is 49 business days, or approximately 10 weeks.

First-Pass Yield. The team quantified the overall quality performance of the value stream. For their purposes they used a measure of first pass yield (FPY). One way of describing this measure is that it reflects the probability that a job will go through all process steps without encountering a quality related problem. They calculated the overall FPY by multiplying together the individual quality measures recorded for each process box (see Table 6-1).

Table 6-1. First-Pass Yield (FPY)

Process	Quality Measure
Enter order % C&A	0.60 (60%)
Generate drawings % C&A	0.95 (95%)
Generate BOM % C&A	1.00 (100%) (*)
Fabricate yield	.99 (99%)
Finish yield	.99 (99%)
Assemble yield	.99 (99%)
Assemble % C&A	.80 (80%) (*)
Invoice adjustments (1.6%)	.984 (98%)
First-Pass Yield	**.44 (44%)**

* You typically find bill-of-material (BOM) errors at the assemble operation.
Therefore, we show it in the data box (and on the table above) for assemble.

By adding the information from Steps 5 and 6 to the map the team has now completed ABC's site-level current state map (see Figures 6-6A and 6-6B).

Reflecting on the Current State Map

Once a team draws a map documenting and measuring the value streams, it should reflect on what the map tells them about these streams. We suggest using questions like the ones in the following box to document the team's conclusions. The team can then use this feedback to help build its future state map. In the next chapter, we look at how some lean concepts can improve a value stream design.

Current State Map Reflection Discussion

- What do you see?

- Where is the process broken, and why?

- Where are queues of information or material forming? Where does batch processing occur? What are some of the possible root causes?

- Is there any evidence of "pushing" the processing of information or materials before the next step is ready for it?

- Where is there a lack of standardized work, places where people perform particular activities in different ways?

- Are the various information technologies adequately integrated?

- Is the work prioritized consistently and in a way that makes sense?

The ABC Design team had these observations during its current state reflection:

- Lead times are long for the processes outside production.

- There is a lot of paperwork inventory in queue in different areas holding up information and jobs.

- The overall quality of the value stream is low because people in different functions don't appear to understand what other departments expect of them in order to do their work efficiently.

- A lot of paperwork is being sent around in support of just one order per day.

- Different technologies supporting different functions are creating a lack of data connectivity and possible workarounds.

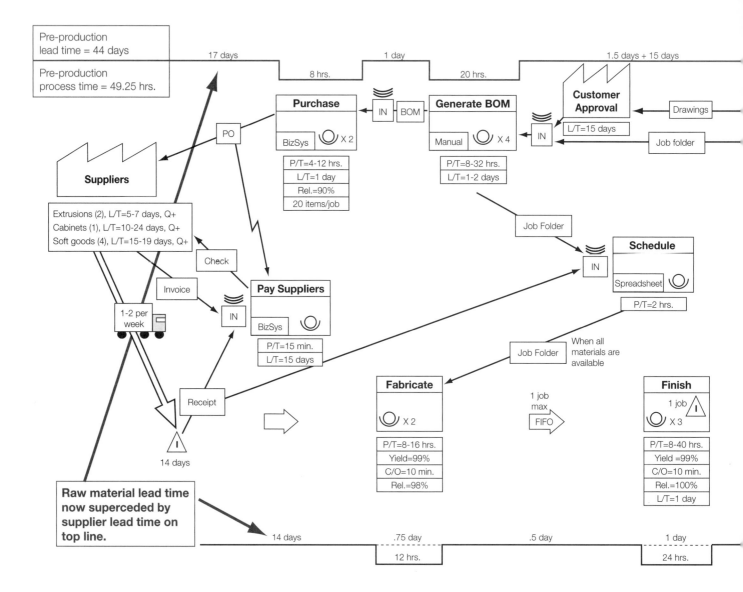

Figure 6-6A. Work Prioritization and Summary Metrics Added (Steps 5 and 6)

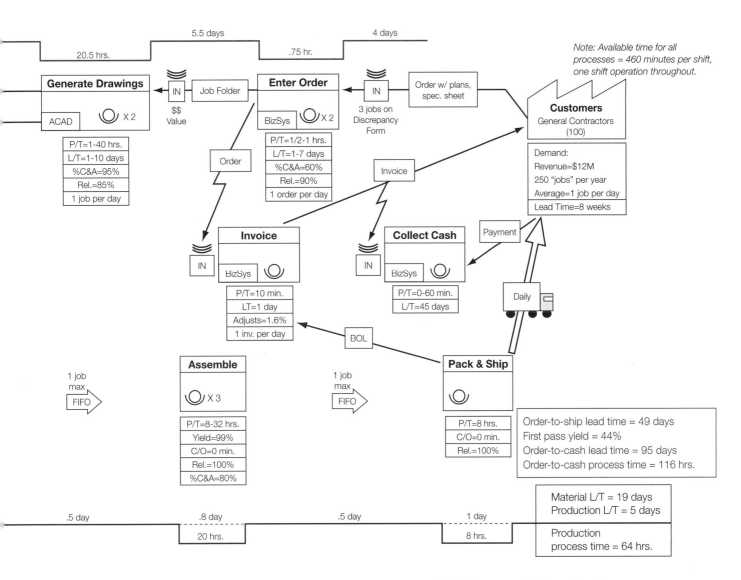

Figure 6-6B. Work Prioritization and Summary Metrics Added (Steps 5 and 6) (*continued*)

CHAPTER 7

Thinking Lean at the Functional Level

A lean enterprise is market driven and customer-oriented, which means the company must design its future state to meet the needs of the market in an effective and efficient manner. To this end, a company must challenge all current business practices and improve them by implementing lean principles and practices. Of course, one of the key concepts of lean thinking is systematically eliminating waste during a lean implementation. However, a company needs to be aware of two important points.

First, a company cannot eliminate or even reduce waste if it means jeopardizing its ability to meet customer needs and improve its competitive advantage. While this point seems obvious, some companies fail to keep this in mind throughout various improvement efforts.

Second and less obvious is that wastes typically exist in the company's current system for particular reasons. The team needs to use lean tools to identify and address the *root causes* of these wastes, not the *symptoms*, or the company will never permanently eliminate or reduce waste (see Figure 7-1). In the past, a company may have established specific business practices to meet particular business needs that are no longer valid. We call these legacy systems. The company may have put in place seemingly complicated practices because it could not identify simpler approaches at the time, or before the availability of new tools and technologies. Companies that fail to address these two points usually fail to complete true site-level value stream maps before initiating their lean transformation. This can set the company up for possible failure from the outset.

To help the company address these points and expand its lean approach to the office, we have developed several questions to help it think lean at the functional level. (Though these questions address the functional levels of a

Figure 7-1. Identifying Root Causes of Visible Waste

process, the team should also use them from the site-level value stream perspective.) Of course, lean transformations require systems thinking. Yet most organizations are accustomed to optimizing jobs within departments, as opposed to optimizing departmental support within the framework of an extended value stream. The questions in this chapter are intended to upset this job optimization mindset by challenging how the current work within the company's value streams actually influences the performance of the enterprise. These various functional-level questions should help managers and team members see the many tangled webs and legacies embedded in the status quo, as well as challenge them to see the office from a lean perspective. The questions are grouped by function in the following sections.

Sales, Marketing, and Operations

Many companies give incentives to their sales departments to sell products and services without regard to how this type of sales activity affects the company's value streams. This often creates tensions among the sales, marketing, and operations departments. As the company puts lean practices in place, the traditional adversarial interactions among sales, marketing, and operations is transformed into an effective team of people who understand the systems level capabilities of a lean enterprise, and the market it serves. The role of sales will change from just selling to the role of customer management—balancing the true needs of the customer with the company's actual operational capabilities. The importance of marketing generally increases in a lean enterprise since its main role is to develop effective and timely tools to identify changes in the marketplace and the needs of the customer. The following questions will help facilitate a discussion focused on an improved future state.

- What is the value to the organization in having complete and accurate information entering the business (e.g., orders, quotes)?

- What is the cost to the value stream of selling products or services that do not fit well in the production value stream?

- What are the consequences to the organization of making commitments, such as ship dates, that are not realistic?

- What is the impact on the effectiveness of sales and marketing if the company reduces the number of product variations?

- What causes the "unlevel" demand (e.g., month-end spikes) shown in Figure 7-2? How does this affect the performance of the organization?

- How much waste would the organization be able to eliminate if sales and marketing worked with operations, as a team?

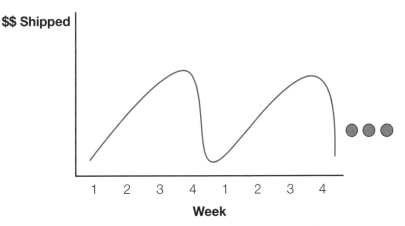

Figure 7-2. Month-end Demand Spikes Cause Problems Throughout the Company

Lean Note: James Womack and Daniel Jones, in their book *Seeing the Whole* (2002), touched on the unlevel demand phenomenon and coined a term, "demand amplification." They identified inaccuracy of information (i.e., forecasts) throughout the supply chain as one of the root causes of this unlevel demand. Inaccurate information often has a snowball or bullwhip effect backward through the supply chain. However, there are other potential causes of unlevel demand. At one company, spikes in demand were related to the timing of pricing changes.

Lean Example: At a printing company with lead times of three to five days, a representative from sales attends at least one of the four operation meetings that occur daily to get updates of current capacity-related information. Perhaps four-color capacity is available in the next several days. Sales can then focus its efforts on potential jobs that fall into this category. In this example, sales is better balancing the needs of the market to the operational capabilities at the time. Of course, commitment and discipline to the practices described are required, but the result is a win-win situation for both the sales and operations functions.

Order Processing

Order processing is the point at which many companies have sales personnel "throwing orders over the wall" to a sequence of internal handoffs before the order reaches the shop floor. Implicit in this legacy is the confusion caused with these handoffs throughout the enterprise. For this function, the company must focus on improving information quality (completeness and accuracy) and timeliness to get the appropriate information to the floor as soon as possible. To facilitate new actions, the team should ask the following questions:

- What would be the consequences of eliminating order entry for some or all value streams?

- How can you reduce the number of order entry transactions and ease the impact of the volume on the rest of the value stream?

- What is the negative impact of incomplete or inaccurate information originating from order entry?

- Can you eliminate manual interfaces by some means such as electronic data interchange or automatic retrieval of quotes?

- What would be the effect of reducing the skills required to perform order processing using work simplification and standardization?

- What would be the impact of greater teamwork between the functional areas involved in order processing? Or, possibly co-locating all the requisite functions (see Figure 7-3)?

Lean Example: Sometimes there is an opportunity for a company to co-locate the various functions responsible for order processing activities physically in one location rather than in different areas or facilities. Bringing together individuals from order entry, engineering or technical support, to form customer service teams to handle all aspects of order processing will dramatically reduce its lead time. The results have been significant in most cases—a 50 percent or greater reduction in lead time.

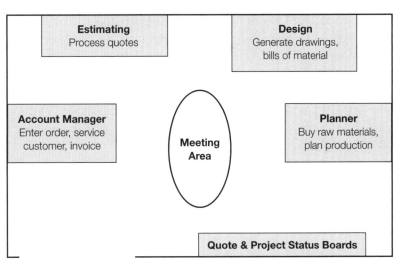

Figure 7-3. Office Cell Example—Order Processing

New Product Design

Discussed as "problem solving" by James Womack and Daniel Jones, new product design is beyond the scope of this workbook, but we do want to provide a few thoughts. Many companies have bad filters or triggers for initiating designs: Inputs and information are kept in silos, resulting in poor choices or extended design cycles with more iterative learning than necessary. In addition, designs are typically passed onto others without understanding the capability of operations and the supply base to produce the new product. The company's lean efforts in the design function should focus on reducing the overall lead time of the design cycle and providing new designs that reflect the capability of the extended value streams. Asking the following questions can begin discussion on a new way of acting:

- Would the quality and quantity of the design activity be improved by a better filter of projects? If so, what would be the impact on R&D capacity and the rest of the value stream?

- What wastes could be eliminated downstream if designs were not "thrown over the wall" to the next function (e.g., purchasing, production)?

- What would be the value stream impact of improving the process and lead time of the iterations involved in designing new products?

- What wastes can you eliminate by using standardized work throughout the design process?

- What will be the effect on lead time if the appropriate design tools are made available to designers and engineers as well as fully utilized by them?

- Can you reduce batch sizes in the design process? In other words, can you release smaller design elements to the next process in order to improve flow, decrease quality problems, and achieve the other benefits of smaller batch processing, such as leveling?

- Is design capacity adequately understood and planned? How much time do engineering resources spend on nondesign-related activities?

Lean Example: A company involved in the design of machine tooling decided to take a very different approach to tool design in order to meet the market's request for shorter lead time. In the past, a tool designer would be assigned to a project, responsible for all aspects from beginning to end. Tool designers worked a single shift each day, leaving the project every evening to resume work the next day. Instead, the company established a two-shift tool design operation. Projects would be shared between two or more designers, and smoothly handed off at the end of each shift. This required a great deal of standardized work to be effective. The result was the reduction in design lead time by greater than 50 percent, as well as improved quality of the design as a result of having another set of eyes involved.

Inventory Control

Inventory control has become a resource-intensive activity because companies have so much inventory to control in a push system! The company's lean efforts here should focus on reducing the level of activity associated with maintaining control of inventory as it implements flow, pull, and leveling concepts on the shop floor. The questions to ask are:

- What inventory control activities will be required as you greatly reduce inventory through the application of lean concepts (e.g., applying flow and pull)?

- How can you simplify inventory control through the visual organization of materials at point of use?

- What is the impact of smaller, more frequent deliveries from suppliers on inventory control activities?

- Are there better ways to control inventory that require less effort while providing the desired results?

- What will be the impact of reduced inventory-related transactions on the quality of data and information?

- What will be the affect of reducing reliance on computer-based methods to control inventory?

Lean Note: Some companies have instituted bar code and scanning technology to automate inventory control-related transactions. While this can sometimes improve the accuracy of the transaction, the transaction still exists, often creating new work associated with maintaining the bar code system (e.g., the printing and distribution of bar codes). As a result, it may not be a true lean improvement. In lean enterprises, companies have reduced the number of inventory-related transactions by as much as 75 percent from that of traditional companies. Only after reducing these transactions do lean enterprises consider automating them.

Purchasing and Inventory Management

Purchasing's legacy in many companies has become a combination of sourcing new parts to the lowest bidder, pressuring suppliers for cost reductions, and replenishing raw materials when told to do so by the Materials Requirement Planning (MRP)/Enterprise Resource Planning (ERP) system. In a lean enterprise, the focus of purchasing (e.g., buyers, material planners) and inventory management personnel shifts to (1) developing long-term relationships with capable suppliers, (2) sourcing suppliers based on the full costs of purchased parts, and (3) modifying inventory levels in the pull system to reflect changes in market demand or production performance. The questions to ask are:

- What effect will the use of pull/kanban material replenishment systems have on the purchasing and inventory management activity?

- What is the value of developing strategic partnerships with vendors, as opposed to selecting suppliers solely on the basis of price?

- What activities will change with the incorporation of vendor-managed inventories?

- How can you use the newly available time of purchasing and inventory management personnel to improve supplier management?

- What is the impact on the value stream if you eliminate purchase orders or replace them with blanket order agreements?

Lean Example: One company has set up its supplier to dial in several times a day to get access to the equipment metering fluid levels in storage tanks. Another company is making use of the Internet and a web cam to review current inventory levels that are physically sitting on the customer's shelves. In both cases, it is the supplier having access to the appropriate information that determines for them what materials to send and in what amount.

Scheduling and Production Control

The heartbeat of the legacy ERP/MRP production system resides in scheduling and production control. This function attempts to minimize the chaos on the floor by gathering information from all points in the plant, which enables damage control. As the company's lean efforts significantly reduce overall lead time, the focus of this group should shift to regulating the pace of flexible production through leveling the mix and volume of production jobs. The following questions help determine alternate approaches to scheduling and production control:

- How will regular production meetings change as a result of implementing flow and pull systems?

- What changes will be required to existing scheduling systems (manual or computer-based) to support smaller increments of work flowing through the operation?

- What will be the effect on scheduling activities of a more level volume and mix of products flowing through the operation?

- What will be the effect on scheduling the value stream if the company does not initiate work until all resources such as materials, instructions, and drawings are available?

- How will you simplify the scheduling and production control activities as the company reduces production lead time?

- What is the impact on the value stream of a significant reduction in the number of rush orders?

Lean Example: One company practically eliminated rush orders when it reduced the production lead time from five weeks to one day. This greatly reduced the amount of expediting effort required to maintain customer service. Unfortunately, rush orders are a dysfunction that companies have come to live with—a necessary evil of conducting business. However, the cost to the company of such a high level of expediting can be significant.

Quality Management

Several industries require significant effort in quality system reporting as a customer requirement (e.g., defense contracting, good manufacturing practices in food and drug industries). Many companies have created quality systems based on individual, narrow interpretations of these guidelines. The company needs to be creative and challenge these interpretations to reduce product lead time and cost. Therefore, the focus is on minimizing the effort required to meet such requirements while maximizing the benefits of a well-designed quality management system. Questions to challenge the current state in quality management include:

- How will the implementation of flow and standardized work affect the existing quality system?

- What activities change with the application of quality-at-the-source concepts on and off the production floor?

- What is the impact of current quality management-related activities on the lead time and cost of the product?

- Are the current quality system guidelines reflecting true customer quality requirements for the value stream?

- Does the quality management system provide timely and accurate information that drives continuous improvement?

Lean Example: A company in the pharmaceutical industry used 28 inspectors throughout the organization to inspect batch-related quality documentation, requiring five days to review, reconcile, and close out quality records for each batch processed prior to shipment. By challenging existing forms and manual reporting processes, the company reduced the effort associated with this activity by 75 percent. In addition, the company reduced the lead time for the closeout process from five days to one.

Cost Accounting

The intention of most cost accounting systems is to track and report product costs and compare them to expectations such as standard or quoted costs versus actual costs. Several industries require significant effort in detailed cost reporting as a customer requirement (e.g., government-contracted work). Nevertheless, companies may greatly simplify the process itself, particularly as material flow is improved and work is standardized. The focus of lean efforts in the cost accounting function is to reduce the time and effort needed to collect required data and to transform it to meaningful information. Future state discussions may be enhanced in cost accounting redesigns with these questions:

- How do cost accounting activities change as the company creates flow and standardizes work?

- What is the impact of current cost accounting practices on the value stream (e.g., labor reporting)?

- How would understanding the actual overhead cost in a product family influence strategic and operational decisions?

- Is cost-related information generated on a timely basis in order to effectively support operational decision making?

- How can the cost accountants effectively support the value stream? What analysis can they perform to support decisions on the future state design?

Lean Example: At one company, each production associate spent approximately 30 minutes every eight-hour shift on detailed labor reporting due to the lack of flow: Each area required separate labor reporting. As part of the lean transformation, production cells were established that combined several processes in one area of flow. Upon implementing a production cell, the team reduced time spent on this activity by 80 percent.

General Accounting

The complexity of this legacy reflects the complexity of the production system it supports, and the extensive procedures needed for paperwork systems. In addition, this activity usually works with very large batches of information: A month-end close has a month's worth of transactions (see Figure 7-4)! The lean focus in this area focuses on simplifying work (and reducing batch sizes) in various functions of general accounting, including paying suppliers, invoicing customers, and receiving payment while meeting local, state and federal accounting requirements. Introducing lean concepts and thoughts within general accounting can be facilitated with the following questions:

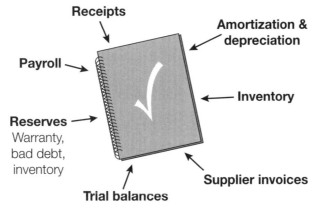

Figure 7-4. Month-End General Accounting Transactions

- What is the time and effort required to perform month-end closing activities throughout the enterprise?

- How will more timely and accurate financial and accounting information help specific processes (e.g., periodic reports), and the organization in general?

- What would be the impact on the accounting function if you simplified labor reporting and improved inventory control, receipt of goods, and shipment of finished product?

- How does the batching of accounting transactions (e.g., invoices, expenses, receipts) affect the ability to manage the value stream, or the organization as a whole?

- How does the practice of three-way matching, such as purchase order, receipt, and supplier invoice, affect cost and transaction lead time?

- What would be the impact to the organization if the accounting function reduced its portion of the order-to-cash lead time?

Lean Example: One company expended long hours to complete month-end closing. This periodic ritual took as much as two weeks to complete as accounting personnel pulled together the necessary data from various sources. By reducing batch practices of related transactions and standardizing work, they were able to reduce month-end close to a four-hour process. The goal is to close daily with very small batches of transactions!

Human Resources

Traditional companies often spend too much time on the administrative tasks of hiring, payroll, and benefits, resulting in a functional area that doesn't understand how to support the growth and retention of the work force. The lean focus in this area is to simplify the administrative activities and enhance the ability to grow, train, and retain flexible employees. The following questions will challenge the way human resources functions and will help design new value streams to support the organization:

- What would be the benefit of reducing the effort associated with payroll-related activities such as processing and correcting time cards?

- What would be the impact to the organization on employee retention of improving the screening, hiring, and orienting processes?

- What is the cost associated with employee turnover? What is the financial benefit of improved retention?

- What would be the benefit to the organization of simpler, more frequent employee reviews focused on value stream performance?

- How can you change compensation practices to reinforce lean behaviors such as teamwork, standardized work, and cross-training?

- How does standardized work throughout the organization change or alter the training of new employees?

These lean questions should help the value-mapping team generate discussions and ideas, challenge all current business practices, and help focus the team, management, and organization on implementing lean principles and practices that will improve the company's competitive posture. Without such a broad organizational commitment to changing how it does business, the company puts the lean transformation at risk, as well as hampers its efforts to move from the current state to a future state.

CHAPTER 8

Designing a Future State

While the current state map documents the performance in the existing enterprise, the future state map is the opportunity for management to re-define the enterprise to meet specific business objectives concerning the cost, service, and/or quality as perceived by the market. The mapping team may expose many enterprise opportunities during the current state mapping effort, but an organization typically doesn't have all the resources necessary to address all opportunities at once. So, the question becomes: How and where do we start?

Management's best starting point is to focus on those portions of the enter-prise value stream that are directly responsible for selling, designing, and delivering goods and services to the market. Of course, there may be good reason to begin elsewhere in the enterprise value stream. Perhaps the most visible and costly opportunity is somewhere else in the order-to-cash value stream, or some other value stream might be negatively affecting customer perceptions, such as warranty lead times, invoice processing, or excessive documentation.

> *Mapping Tip:* When designing a future state, the mapping team will always uncover several alternatives—there is no single correct future state. However, the team can narrow its selection by designing a future state that directly applies to the business goals of the enterprise, and that the company can implement in a reasonable time frame (typically three to six months).

To begin designing the organization's future state, the team should revisit the initial business objectives and review the current state map along with the reflections resulting from it. We then suggest that the team follow the set of future-state questions in the following box as a guideline to developing a future state. Collectively, the questions represent a thought process that will guide the team in identifying the opportunities to apply lean concepts throughout the organization. Each of the questions is discussed in the following sections. We will then apply these questions to ABC Design in Chapter 9.

Future State Questions

1. What does the customer really need?

2. How often will performance be checked?

3. Which steps create value and which generate waste?

4. How can work flow with fewer interruptions?

5. How will work be controlled between interruptions?

6. How will the workload and/or activities be balanced?

7. What process improvements will be necessary to achieve the future state?

Question 1: What Does the Customer Really Need?

Since lean is market driven, it's not surprising that we begin with asking this question. The following questions dig deeper and provide a more thoughtful response from the team:

- Who needs the output of the process?

- What is specifically required? How often is it required?

- When do they need the output?

In other words, what specifically does the customer want and by when do they want it? What is the required service level for the process—the desired response or turnaround time? Perhaps the company needs to enter all orders within one hour of receipt to support a particular goal for overall order-process lead time. This would then define the desired service level for the company's particular customer.

Further, what is the expected quality level of the output? Organizations typically have established quality standards in production processes. However, often in office processes organizations do not clearly know the quality requirements. Determining this quality level is important when checking performance, which is discussed later in this chapter.

For value streams that are transaction driven the team can also ask:

- What is the demand rate for the process? How much of the output is required over what period of time?

- How much does the demand vary over time?

- What resources will the organization require to meet the various demand rates?

In other words, just as it does for production, the organization needs to know what the takt time is for transactional office processes. Takt time synchronizes the pace of processing to match the pace of customer need or demand. That is, it is the rate for completing work based on customer need. Takt time is defined as:

$$\text{Takt Time} = \frac{\text{Effective working time per time period}}{\text{Customer requirement during the time period}}$$

Let's say that in a single shift the organization can receive 46 orders. Order entry personnel work an 8-hour shift, with 30 minutes for lunch and two 10-minute breaks. Therefore, their effective working time per shift is 460 minutes. The takt time is:

$$\text{Takt Time} = \frac{460 \text{ minutes per shift}}{46 \text{ orders per shift}} \text{ or } 10 \text{ minutes per order}$$

Ideally, order entry personnel should be entering one order every 10 minutes in a smooth and continual manner. Further, if the process time to enter an order is 20 minutes per order, then the company must provide two people to perform the order entry process to meet demand:

$$\frac{\text{Process time of 20 minutes per person per order}}{\text{Takt time of 10 minutes per order}} = \frac{20}{10} \text{ or } \begin{array}{c}\text{2 people required} \\ \text{to do the work}\end{array}$$

In this way, the company can ensure that it is providing sufficient capacity to meet demand.

It is often necessary for the mapping team to define several takt times for the company's administrative processes. For instance, when resources are shared across product or service families, the overall demand on a particular process must be determined in order to calculate the appropriate takt time. In addition, a company can sometimes express demand in different work units that are meaningful to a process. Orders per day may make sense for an order entry process, while line items per day may make sense for a purchasing process. Companies can also creatively define demand in ways that are meaningful for establishing takt time, such as expressing takt time in terms of dollars or time (e.g., labor hours required).

Understanding customer requirements, including takt times, is important as the team identifies an appropriate management time frame for the various processes within the enterprise. In addition, understanding the resource requirements for each activity may lead the company to discuss new roles and responsibilities in order to improve flow, which is discussed later in this chapter.

Question 2: How Often Will Performance Be Checked?

Once the team establishes customer requirements, it is important to check the performance of this work against these requirements. There's a fundamental reason for this: If the company designs a system to perform to customer requirements, it will need to check for abnormalities that hinder this performance and then create corrective actions (countermeasures) to get the work back on track.

So what is a reasonable management time frame, or "pitch," for this activity? In an office environment, it can be somewhat arbitrary. Let's go back to the order entry process example, where the takt time is 10 minutes. Since the company may not receive one order every 10 minutes, management may establish a service level (which can be used as an alternative to takt time) of having all orders entered within one hour of receipt. How long does the organization want to wait before it determines whether it is processing orders in a timely manner? Management would certainly not wait until the end of the day to discover that there is a problem—valuable time would be lost forever. Nor would they want to check performance every increment of takt time (every 10 minutes). In this case, management might select one hour as a reasonable time frame to check performance in order entry.

As the team thinks through new lean behaviors, it shouldn't spend a lot of time checking the performance of the system. Instead, it can determine ways to use simple and visual means of checking performance called takt image. Companies have developed creative visual means to provide takt image on a variety of administrative processes. In the order entry example, the mapping team could easily establish some simple visual means to determine the age of an order at a glance using timed in-boxes, color, or some other technique (see Figure 8-1).

What happens if the order entry personnel are not processing orders in a timely manner within a particular one-hour period? The team must quickly

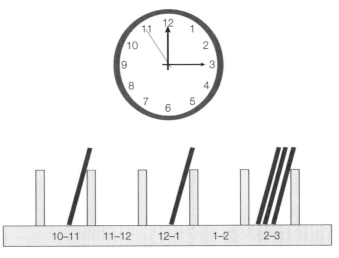

Figure 8-1. A Visual Means to Check Performance

identify the root causes and immediately take corrective actions to return to the desired service level. For instance, if a spike occurred in the number of orders received, the company could bring additional resources from other areas to meet this temporary change in demand. Alternatively, if order entry receives an order with incomplete and inaccurate information, someone could quickly follow up with the customer to resolve the problem while the system performance is kept intact.

Lean Example: A printing company developed a goal of a three-day turnaround on orders, with a one-day turnaround in the preproduction portion of the order. They decided on a two-hour management time frame to review the preproduction process, such as customer service, artwork, and plate making. Every two hours representatives from each area reviewed the orders-in-process to determine if they were meeting service levels at each stage. If they were not, they took corrective action by releasing work to the next stage and redeploying resources (workers), as necessary. The review took about five minutes to perform, taking up only 20 minutes per shift—a small price to pay to ensure the company's competitive performance.

Lean Example: The engineering manager at one company wanted to improve flow and reduce lead time of the design process. In the past, the manager would hold meetings every two weeks to determine the status of the various design efforts in process. However, scheduled completion dates continued to slip. To correct this, the manager determined the takt time in terms of engineering hours required per period (e.g., per week). Then he broke demand down into blocks of time that related to actual deliverable items, such as drawings. Finally, he established a management time frame of two days, meaning each engineer had a specific task assigned that had to be completed in two days. The manager reviewed progress every two days to determine if the engineers were meeting the service level. If not, the manager took corrective action such as reassigning resources or tasks to keep the value stream performance on track.

Question 3: Which Steps Create Value and Which Generate Waste?

All enterprises have tasks or processes that only add cost and time to its services and products. To root these wastes out the team should challenge the work in a value stream by asking questions such as:

- What does the customer really need?

- Why are the current steps being performed?

- What can the company do differently or not at all while still meeting customer needs?

- Is the order of steps creating waste? At what steps should decisions be made?

- What assumptions underlie the design of the current process?

- Are current controls and administrative guidelines appropriate?

- What knowledge and skills are truly required to perform the steps?

What does the customer really need? If in doubt, ask the customer. Maybe the customers don't need some of the work at all! By verifying the needs of the customer, examining the current steps, and identifying wastes, the team focuses the discussion on emphasizing the tasks that support requirements and eliminating activities that have no bearing on requirements.

It might be important to unravel the history of the existing system to identify the particular rules and assumptions that underlie the current structure. For example, the company may have set up a system to accommodate the skill level of particular individuals that it no longer employs. On the other hand, there could be an assumption that the management information system can only work a certain way, and the company designed the process around this limitation. Meanwhile, a subsequent version of the software had corrected the problem. In some cases, current practices are a result of administrative controls the company established in the past. Is there still a need for them? What are their costs versus their perceived benefits?

Another area of non-value-adding activity is relying on a high level of skills to perform a task when lesser skills might be possible (or vice versa!). There may be a means to simplify and standardize an activity so other or fewer people can perform it. Information system-based solutions and technologies may eliminate reliance on the specialized information that certain employees possess to execute the current system–or what's called tribal knowledge. The organization might be able to eliminate entire processes or at least automate them by the application of such solutions.

Question 4: How Can Work Flow with Fewer Interruptions?

Many shop floors are benefiting from the concept of one-piece flow or continuous flow, where work progresses from task to task without queues. Most companies don't consider flow in office work, and assume batch processing is a normal business practice in the office. This results in sending piles of work downstream, over the wall to the next process, which creates long lead times for the office value streams (see Figure 8-2).

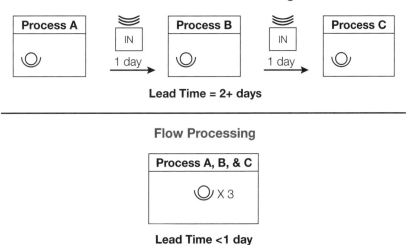

Figure 8-2. From Batch and Queue to Flow Processing

Companies may have valid reasons (known as root causes) for batch processing, such as office equipment availability, or people supporting several value streams. Challenging the barriers to flow and creating smaller batches of work focuses an enterprise's efforts on improving cost, service, and quality. Figure 8-3 demonstrates the positive effect of smaller batch processing on the value stream.

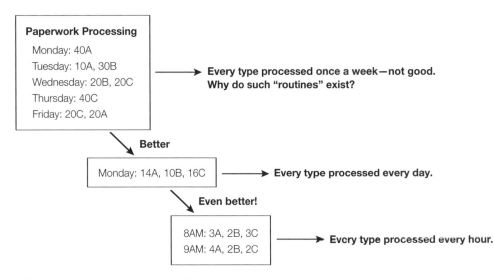

Figure 8-3. Approaching One-Piece Flow with Smaller Batches (derived from *Learning to See,* V1.2, p. 52)

Referring to Figure 8-3, let's say that A, B, and C are different types of paperwork or administrative processes (e.g., invoices, receipts, and general ledger). Just like the production area, ideal one-piece-flow is not always possible in some nonproduction processes, but it is still better to process smaller batches at a time, resulting in reduced lead time, and other desirable outcomes like improved flexibility. Certainly, creating an invoice every hour is better than once a week. The team must identify and resolve any existing barriers to smaller batches. Therefore, the question remains as to what the appropriate batch size is. In other words, how much work should be triggered: A week's worth? A day's worth? Or an hour's worth? Of course, the trigger should be developed in concert with the desired management time frame or "pitch" as well as any necessary service levels.

Many industries have realized the significant benefits of uninterrupted flow by establishing multifunctional administrative teams organized in production-like cells in such processes as customer service (e.g., from order to invoice), order processing (e.g., design-to-order), product design (e.g., concurrent engineering), bidding and proposal teams, warehouse and distribution, and contract administration (see Figure 8-4). By incorporating the flow strategy, these companies have seen such tangible benefits as reduced lead time, improved quality, and greater flexibility.

For example, when looked at from the various customers' viewpoints, it becomes clear that companies typically organize maintenance departments by trade or skill, not by service families. Using value stream management concepts, companies can easily identify service families in its future state that dedicated maintenance personnel can support. The future state might include service families such as building and grounds, production support

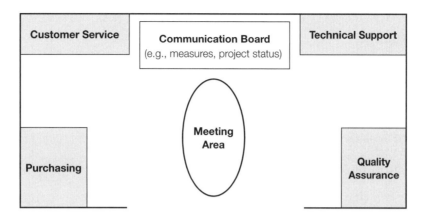

Figure 8-4. A Multifunctional Administrative Team Cell

(e.g., preventive and reactive maintenance), project support (e.g., product and process development, equipment rebuild). Where appropriate, companies could also assign people with various skills or trades (e.g., electrician, plumber, or mechanic) to a service family. These new value streams could result in greatly improved maintenance support.

> *Lean Example:* A distribution operation printed "pick lists" for customer orders every evening for the next day. The company decided to print customer orders more frequently—every two hours. This allowed the company to improve its service to its customers and offer same-day shipping of orders received before 3:00 P.M. The company selected a pitch of 30 minutes. They reviewed the system every 30 minutes to verify that it was meeting the goals established.

> *Lean Example:* One trucking company processes an average of 10,000 pieces of mail per week. The company successfully applied one-piece flow concepts to the processing of mail with a 60 percent reduction in lead time and a 90 percent improvement in process quality. One of the major improvements was correctly matching, sorting, and organizing paperwork.

It is clear that by applying flow concepts to office processes, companies can reduce lead time, increase responsiveness, and improve the quality of the office value streams. Following are some questions the team can ask to determine how they can design better flow in value streams:

- What administrative roles could the company change?

- Can standardizing work impact flow?

- Is it beneficial to dedicate resources to specific tasks or even particular value streams?

- Is it possible to cross-train one person to perform several sequential tasks?

- Is it possible to move people and tasks together in a cell to process work without delay?

- What would be the benefits and issues of a flow approach?

Of course, such a discussion might generate anxiety among functional representatives. Referring to the current state map may provide a context for this discussion to take place.

Question 5: How Will Work Be Controlled Between Interruptions?

Office work typically progresses through a value stream with each step "throwing it over the wall" to the next step. In many cases, the person receiving this work might not be available or be overwhelmed with other work, resulting in the work being queued in an in-box. We call this type of progression a push system, similar to that found on many shop floors.

Flow relieves this issue, as the company finds ways to combine tasks and/or people to allow work to progress without queues. However, there are times when flow is not possible: The person receiving the work might be responsible for tasks outside the value stream, or might be located some distance away. It makes sense to find a way to smooth the impact of interrupted flow to improve the system performance. By establishing simple and visual rules, companies can prevent one part of the value stream from getting too far ahead of another. That is, instead of pushing information forward it's possible to pull it forward, allowing work to progress only when the next step is ready for it.

One method that utilizes the concept of pull is a FIFO (first-in, first-out) lane. As we discussed in Chapter 4 in dealing with overproduction on the shop floor, FIFO lanes not only prioritize what work to do next, but also establish a maximum amount of work that can be queued between tasks. For instance, if there was a FIFO lane allowing five orders to queue between two process steps, Step A could not work on any more orders if there were already five orders in the FIFO lane (see Figure 8-5). The person would either find something else to do or assist the person at Step B to move the work along the value stream. This is considered a pull because Step A can't move work forward without Step B being ready for it, eliminating overproduction from

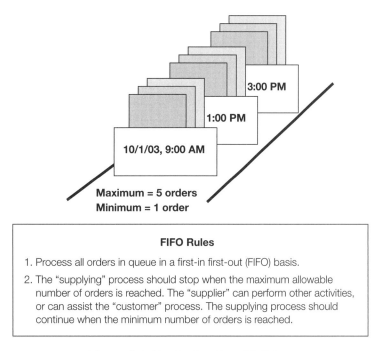

Maximum = 5 orders
Minimum = 1 order

FIFO Rules

1. Process all orders in queue in a first-in first-out (FIFO) basis.

2. The "supplying" process should stop when the maximum allowable number of orders is reached. The "supplier" can perform other activities, or can assist the "customer" process. The supplying process should continue when the minimum number of orders is reached.

Figure 8-5. First-In-First-Out (FIFO) Lane

Step A. Of course, there is a small queue of work, which can ebb and flow to a maximum of five orders.

Another example of pull is to print information only upon demand, allowing modifications and updates to occur without affecting the downstream process. For example, modifications to engineering drawings have less impact on purchasing if they are printed out only when purchasing is ready to act on the drawing. Customer orders can also change frequently in many businesses: Management can apply simple and visual pull concepts to minimize the impact of these changes, only printing the information when someone is ready to process the order.

By using pull systems with visual signals that trigger work, the company can support teams in meeting their objectives, and assist with the reallocation of resources to make sure that people are working on the right thing at the right time. Companies in various industries have successfully applied pull concepts to administrative processes including, but not limited to: order processing, product design, work-order generation, accounting, human resources, purchasing, pick and pack operations, and job packet creation in a job shop environment.

Lean Example: Job shops often use job packets throughout production to make certain that the product is made correctly. At one company, the office released job packets to the floor as soon as possible, creating overproduction. Production began work on many of these released packets and spent a great deal of time reacting to customer changes while the open orders were on the floor. The company implemented a simple pull system for job packets by having production tell the office when it needed the next job packet. The company reduced the number of job packets in the shop by 50 percent, and reduced the number of time-consuming changes to job packets by 80 percent.

Question 6: How Will the Workload and/or Activities Be Balanced?

Work typically requires balancing from two perspectives: the process level and the system level. At the process level, there are people who overproduce in big batches, creating queues at the next step. At the system level, there are lopsided transactions and activities (such as month-end activities) that require different amounts of resources at different points in time. Both types of imbalance create serious problems for the value stream as people must make significant adjustments to their daily efforts, and lead times can get very long.

Work at a process level can be balanced inside a value stream by using techniques such as management pitch, cross-training, and FIFO lanes. All of these focus on absorbing and reacting to changes in the work to enable a smooth progression through the value stream. Techniques are also available to balance lopsided work at a system level. Lean thinking refers to this as leveling work, which reduces the system chaos and overtime by distributing the same transactions and work over a longer period. Establishing a consistent flow of transactions and activities creates a very predictable enterprise and improves the visibility and responsiveness to problems and/or minor shifts in customer demand. Determining the correct mix of transactions improves the ability of the system to flow or respond to particular steps—for example, determining the ideal number of rush orders versus standard orders that are processed. In addition, adjusting the volume of transactions (demand variation) can root out inefficiencies in the system (e.g., having to ship much of the product at the end of the quarterly financial period to make the financial numbers).

However, companies must also address the issue of leveling the volume of work at a system level—for example, identifying and correcting root causes for month-end surges, if they exist. For this issue, the mapping team needs to generate creative ideas to level the volume of incoming orders. While there are usually no simple solutions, the team has an opportunity here to realize significant benefits for the company.

Lean Example: The CFO of one company was concerned about the peak demand created in the month-end close process: it was chaotic and absorbed many late hours each month. He suggested that the concept of leveling might be something that would work for him. In fact, the technique worked because there were transactions he could begin well before the end of the month, leveling the peak need of resources. As a result of this leveling, the processing time was reduced by 50 percent at month end.

Question 7: What Process Improvements Will Be Necessary to Achieve the Future State?

This final question focuses on the actual activities necessary to incorporate all the design features for the new future state. Achieving each change to the current state requires an event, or kaizen. Examples of these types of improvements at a process level span the gamut of the tools and techniques comprising the lean toolbox, such as:

- Standardized work.

- Quality at the source.

- Batch-size reduction.

- Layout changes.

- Visual controls.

- Cross-functional teams.

- Error-proofing.

The company will also need other efforts for office improvements at a system level, which might include:

- Creating new performance metrics.

- Reorganizing or realigning portions of the office.

- Quantifying customer requirements.

- Establishing better triggers for initiating work.

Each of these improvements requires a detailed work plan to achieve. This topic is covered in Chapter 10.

CHAPTER 9

Designing ABC's Future State

To see how ABC Design tied its current state opportunities to what the enterprise was trying to accomplish, this chapter examines how ABC designed a future state value stream in context of the lean principles of customer requirements, value versus waste, flow, pull, and leveling, which were discussed in Chapter 8. There are many opportunities and possible future state designs for any given current state: We'll take you through one example at ABC to demonstrate the concept.

The primary reason for ABC mapping the enterprise was the long lead times associated with orders and the resulting 20 percent drop in sales. Typically, a company would begin with creating a future state map for the functions in the enterprise value stream that directly affect enter order through pack and ship lead time. However, since ABC had already made big improvements in the production area, and the mapping team was charged with reducing another four weeks of lead time, the future state discussions in this chapter will focus on the work flow and processes that precede production: enter order through raw material receipt. Now we can see how ABC's mapping team addressed the future state questions and designed a future state map to achieve its business goals.

Assessing Customer Requirements

The first question the ABC mapping team addressed was: *What does the customer really need?* Once the team defined their customer's needs they had to determine what the required service level or desired turnaround time was for the process. In the case of ABC, the market demanded an eight-week lead time for delivery of goods. Since the production and shipping processes required approximately one week, ABC needed to complete its preproduction process within seven weeks. After establishing this goal, the mapping team discussion centered on reviewing the demand on the various preproduction processes to find ways to ensure that the company could maintain sufficient capacity to meet the demand within the shorter lead time.

In ABC's case, the company expected to maintain the same level of business over the next year if it could make changes to reduce overall lead time. The management also felt that describing demand in terms of a job was appropriate throughout the value stream, from Enter Order to Invoice. Therefore, the mapping team calculated takt time (an alternative term for takt time in an office environment is *pace of customer demand*) as follows:

> Available time = 480 minutes per shift less 20 minutes of breaks, or 460 minutes per shift with a one-shift operation throughout.
>
> Demand = 1 job per day.
>
> Takt time = 460 minutes per day / 1 job per day = 460 minutes per job.

This takt time means ABC must be able to process an order every 460 minutes to meet its expected demand. This information allowed the team to check ABC's available capacity in the enterprise to support this demand. When comparing takt time in the focus areas to the various process times on the current state map, the team saw that ABC had a potential capacity issue (i.e., a constraint) at Generate Drawings: While the engineers must complete each order within 460 minutes, they required an average of 20.5 hours (1,230 minutes). The team checked to see if resources were sufficient to meet the demand by dividing the process time by the takt time:

> # of people required = Process time divided by takt time
>
> For generate drawings, the # of people required =
> 1230 minutes per job / 460 minutes per job per person = 2.7 people

However, only two people were available to generate drawings. Further, when the two people had to generate difficult jobs, the process time was as high as 40 hours (2,400 minutes). Therefore, at times the company needed as many as five-plus people performing this process to keep up with demand. Of course, the apparent solution would have been to hire more CAD operators who would require 6 to 12 months to learn the various product lines before they would be proficient. The lean thinking solution is to redesign the value stream to minimize incremental new staffing. At this point, the team noted on the future state map (Figure 9-1A) the need for an initial kaizen described as "reduce drawing lead time" with a goal of no more than two days (i.e., a range of one to two days, with an average of 1.5) and four engineers. ABC could later resolve this problem in several ways, including:

- Simplifying the drawing process to reduce the overall processing time.

- Standardizing work to minimize variations in process time and quality of the drawings.

- Cross-training others to support routine tasks and peak demands.

- Improving quality of the data to minimize the overprocessing waste in follow-ups.

- Improving reliability of the CAD system to minimize interruptions and improve access.

Determining Management Time Frame

Once the mapping team determined the customer needs and service level, it was ready to ask the next question that affected customer requirement performance: *How often will performance be checked?* Given a takt time of 460 minutes—let's just say one day per job—the team along with management decided that an appropriate management time frame would be four hours. In other words, management would review the status of the system every four hours to determine if the company was meeting its service levels at each key process. Using this short time frame, ABC could be more assured that jobs were flowing through the preproduction portion of the value stream as expected. When it was not, ABC could reassign resources as necessary to help ensure that it met this goal. To provide a takt image (the more visual the process the easier it is to check takt time), ABC selected an easy solution for the preproduction paperwork: Each key process would have a designated place for each job in process and it would use visual indicators to provide a status of completion at that step. The visual indicators would show if the job was 25 percent, 50 percent, or 75 percent complete at that stage.

MANAGEMENT NOTE

Meeting frequently to check the status of work enables companies to maintain established service levels. How would the performance of the company change if management created frequent, short meetings to check on the status of work and, when necessary, developed immediate countermeasures to get the performance back on track?

Lean Example: One company used different colored flags to provide a visual status of a particular job. Any person walking through the area had an immediate understanding of the status of any job, at a glance, without disrupting any work.

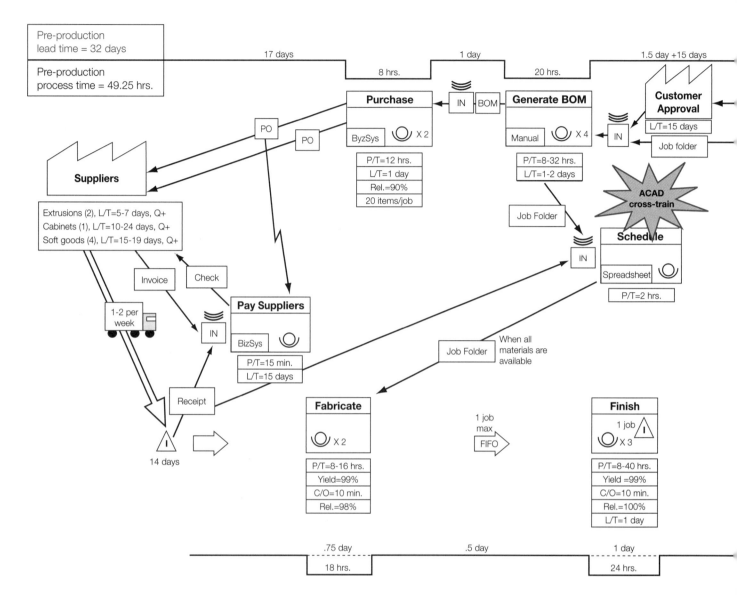

Figure 9-1A. Additions Regarding Customer Requirements and Management Time Frame

Let's understand how this will work. The cycle starts at the beginning of each shift, say 8:00 A.M. At noon, the team reviews each step. The expectation is that each job would be 50 percent complete at this time. Perhaps a job at one step is 75 percent complete, while another job at a different step is lagging behind. The team, recognizing this fact, can redeploy resources accordingly to maintain the flow of orders. To enable this, ABC would need to cross-train its staff; therefore, they added an ACAD cross-train kaizen on the future state map (Figure 9-1A). (The kaizen is usually represented by a red lightning burst. Kaizens are focused improvement efforts that need immediate attention.)

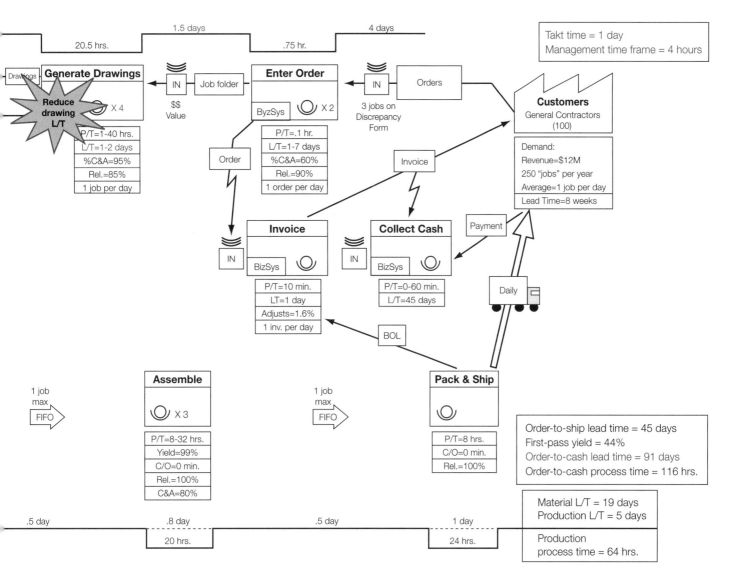

Figure 9-1B. Additions Regarding Customer Requirements and Management Time Frame (*continued*)

Removing Wastes

From a purist point of view, it could be argued that the customer is only concerned with receiving a good design and subsequent products. In the preproduction portion of the value stream, the customer may not care about the process for entering orders, creating BOMs, or purchasing materials. This was a big revelation to ABC management, and it didn't make them very comfortable! It forced them to ask the broader question: *Which steps create value and which generate waste?* The recognition of having to determine waste in this manner helped the mapping team to think out of the box and ask such questions as:

- Is it possible to eliminate or minimize order entry?

- Is it possible to eliminate many BOMs (or reduce their complexity) through more standard products?

- Is it possible to minimize purchasing by standardizing parts and/or reducing the number of suppliers?

- Finally, what might be the impact on the value stream and the current state observations if the mapping team redesigned this portion of the enterprise? Would this be enough to reduce lead time to a competitive level?

Since there are many possible solutions to these problems, we'll just select three process boxes, Enter Order, Generate BOM, and Purchase. We'll discuss one solution for each of them and indicate changes in red. At this stage, the mapping team is exploring an initial future state. However, they can capture any ideal future state concepts for discussion later. We will introduce Figures 9-1A and 9-1B here so you can refer to them as we update the future state map to reflect the decisions of the mapping team and ABC management discussed so far.

Enter Order. While many companies now use web-based orders, ABC didn't have this option because its sales reps weren't ready to make that leap. Though the mapping team couldn't eliminate entering orders inside ABC, they could make use of "quality at the source" and possibly eliminate the lead time and discrepancy reports associated with the 60% C&A quality level at Enter Order. So the team elected to ask the sales reps to call in each order and utilize online order entry to ensure complete and accurate information. The reps could fax the layouts to be included in the job packet. The team also decided to supply the sales reps with a standard checklist to facilitate the entry process. The team added a kaizen for online order entry (Figure 9-2B), with a goal of 100% C&A and a lead time of one day.

> *Ideal State:* The sales rep could design the customer's order with the customer on-line, using a laptop and simultaneously transmitting the information to the business system and CAD.

Generate BOM. ABC's manual effort in this processing area is an example of processing waste. ABC generated the bills-of-material for internal use to trigger the purchasing and production processes. While the company may still need this function in some form, the mapping team decided to reduce the lead time and minimize the processing time by using information technology tools in BizSys and eliminating the manual effort. By incorporating this technology, the mapping team believed that ABC could reduce the effort to two people (from four) and improve the quality of the BOM effort.

> *Ideal State:* ABC could easily see the positive impact on lead time if it enabled the customer to perform online reviews of the drawings, or possibly eliminate reviews altogether through up-front design sessions with the customer and sales reps, resulting in immediate approvals.

At this point, the team put an automated BOMs kaizen on the future state map (Figure 9-2A) with a goal of 100 percent quality, processing time of 8 to 16 hours, and a lead time of one day. What happens to the two people freed up in the BOM area? ABC just found some people to help in the drawing area!

Purchase. Purchasing parts may have several types of waste associated with it: over-processing (redundant parts), waiting (quotes involving unique parts), defects, and so on. ABC was not happy with its processing lead time to Purchase, or their suppliers' lead times associated with some cabinets and soft goods that could be as long as 21 days. The mapping team decided to attack both the suppliers' lead time and ABC's processing time by creating blanket purchase orders for standard parts and standardizing many of the parts that were responsible for the long lead time. This would also give the supplier an opportunity to build some items to stock and cut down lead time.

By incorporating these changes, the mapping team believed the Purchase process time would drop to no more than four hours and lead time could be cut several days for the cabinet and soft goods suppliers, with the longest lead time being 7 to 21 days. At this point, the team put a blanket orders and a standardize parts kaizen on the future state map (Figure 9-2A) with a goal of four-hour purchase processing time and 7 to 21 (cabinets) and 7 to 13 (soft goods) day supplier lead times.

In summary, answering the question *Which steps create value and which generate waste?* for a future state map has many answers. We chose one to discuss, but we're sure you can think of many more.

Flowing Work

When the mapping team asked the question: *How can work flow with fewer interruptions?* they uncovered many possibilities to flow at ABC. This section focuses on the few possibilities that ABC was willing to consider for the first

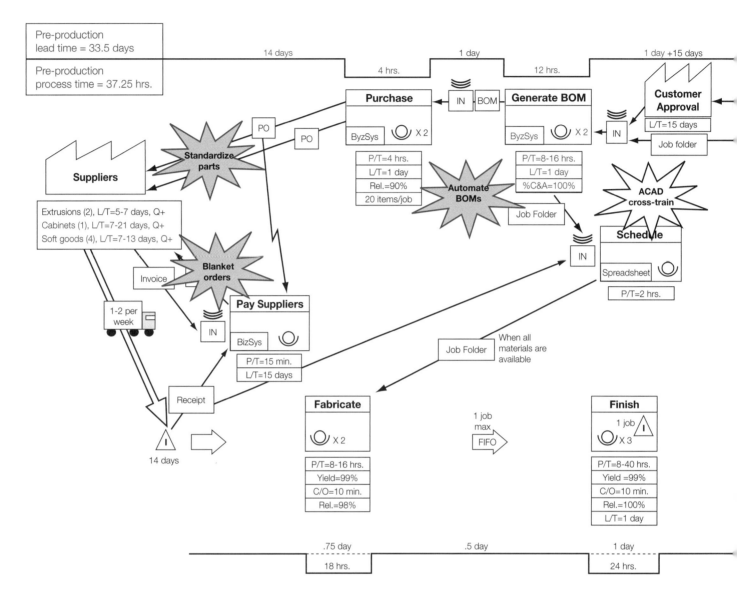

Figure 9-2A. Additions Regarding Removing Wastes

iteration of the future state. We'll introduce Figures 9-3A and 9-3B here so you can refer to it as we add the changes as they occur.

One area that interested ABC managers was the possibility of flowing from Enter Order to Generate Drawings. ABC planned to implement online ordering between the salesperson and order entry. They also thought it might be possible for the sales person to fax the plans to the office at the same time she or he enters the order, allowing the order to be sent to generate drawings as soon as it was completed. Once management saw that possibility, they decided to move Enter Order into Generate Drawings; the

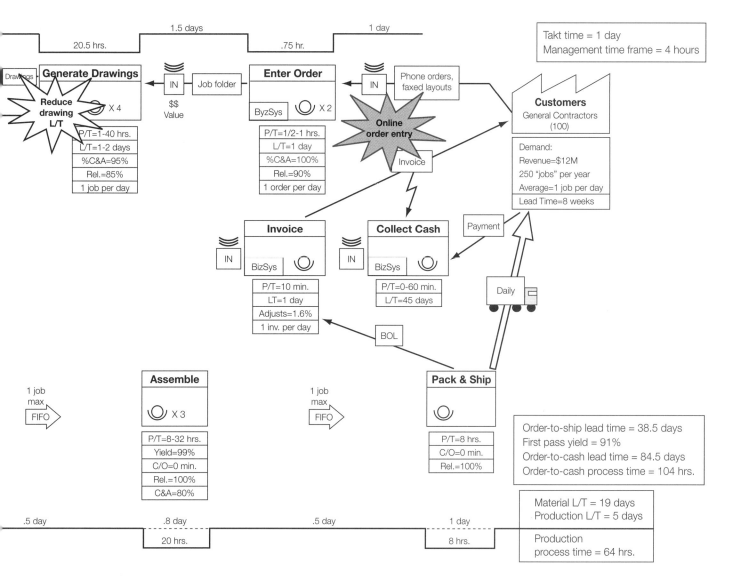

Figure 9-2B. Additions Regarding Removing Wastes (*continued*)

processing time was short, so ABC wanted to use this time to have the engineer enter the order and discuss any technical details with the salesperson. This would require cross-training the engineers in BizSys and the order entry function.

What happened to the two people responsible for entering orders? Based on the data in the current state map, the two people did not enter orders all day long (check the demand of one order a day and the processing time per order). ABC elected to have these people remain in customer service performing their other functions for the time being.

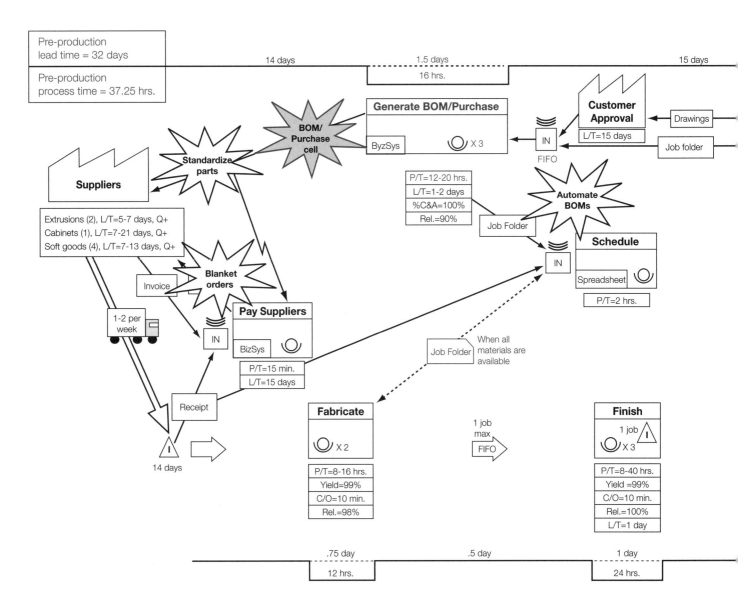

Figure 9-3A. Additions Regarding Flowing Work and Pulling Work

How will this new flow between orders and drawings decrease the lead time? ABC used the two people freed up in generate BOM (due to the automation of bills of material) to increase the number of people generating drawings. They also believed that it was possible to split up the components of the drawing, such as shelves versus cabinets versus cubicles, so that they could work each job in parallel. When the mapping team used the management time frame of four hours to monitor this progress, they believed that they could get a drawing out in one to two days, given the processing time requirements of 1 to 40 hours.

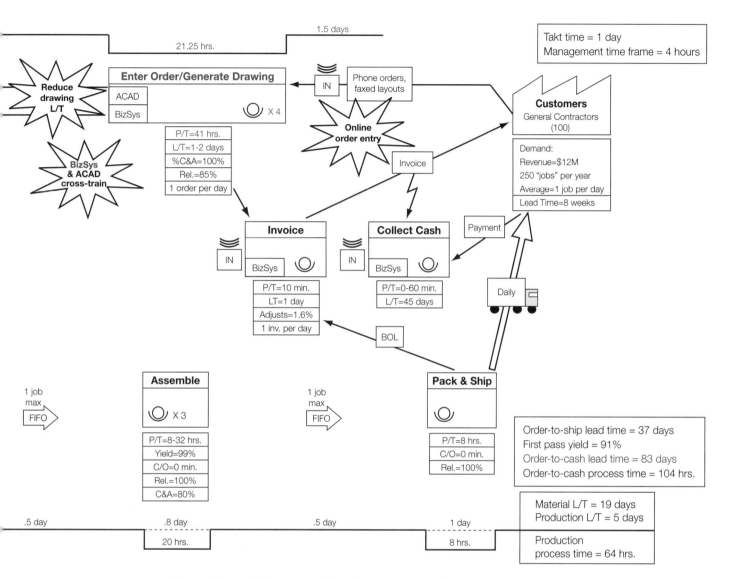

Figure 9-3B. Additions Regarding Flowing Work and Pulling Work (*continued*)

On the future state map 9-3B we documented ABC's new flow by combining the Enter Order and Generate Drawings process boxes, adding both BizSys and ACAD as resident technology, which adds 30 minutes to the processing time, including:

- Absorbing the order entry lead time in flow.

- Splitting up the drawings so it takes no longer than two days to complete each drawing.

Since the necessary kaizens are already drawn on the map (reduce drawing lead time and BizSys cross-train) we don't need to add another kaizen at this point. The mapping team has only clarified what has to be designed within the kaizen.

A second possibility of flow is between the drawing and BOM areas. ABC currently generates drawings and sends them out for approval before generating a BOM. They found out, however, that the customer approvals rarely involve changes affecting the BOM. While this is valuable information to have, ABC still wants to receive a customer approval prior to BOM generation. (Maybe they should address the customer approval lead time in the next future state!)

Another area of flow might be between Generate BOM and purchase. With the improvements we've already discussed for Generate BOM, the new information technology, the blanket orders, and the standardized parts, ABC would like to create a small cell combining the functions (and people) involved in creating BOMs and purchasing parts. However, as we already discussed, ABC would like to begin the BOM prior to receiving the customer approval to reduce the lead time. Is it possible to create a BOM and create purchasing requirements in the cell without obligating ABC to buy the parts? We'll find out with the kaizen the team now places on Figure 9-3A.

Once the ABC mapping team combined the Generate BOM and Purchase process boxes, and changed the data boxes to reflect 12 to 20 hours of processing time and a reduction in lead time of one day, they now had two people purchasing these parts, but only needed four hours of processing time. When ABC dug deeper, they found that both purchasing agents were capable of buying all the necessary parts on the BOM. As a result, they assigned only one agent to the new Generate BOM/Purchase cell to work in parallel with customer approval and had the other continue to support other needs in the company. At this point, the mapping team believed they had done enough improvement in flow for the first round of the future state map, so they moved on to the next question regarding organizing and prioritizing work.

Pulling Work

ABC designed the information flow on the shop floor to direct operators on what task to do next. Most offices, on the other hand, have very informal information flows, making it difficult for office workers to prioritize their work consistently. In ABC's case, one worker may schedule work based on the size of the task, while others may schedule according to the due dates, monetary value of the transaction, standard versus custom work, etc. The information flow in ABC's office is just as important as the one on the shop floor, because both can affect lead time to the customer. Asking, *How will work be controlled between interruptions?* challenged the mapping team with the fact that there was very little volume in the company: only one order a day on average, which could possibly create a need for several drawings and purchasing calls. In the event that several orders came in during a single day, it would be useful to introduce a FIFO rule for prioritization; each document, once it entered the enterprise, was treated in first-in/first out prioritization. ABC could accomplish this by identifying the date or sequence for each job at each desk, allowing workers to immediately choose the next one in line to minimize the leap frog effect of inconsistent priorities. Therefore, it made sense to prioritize the jobs with a pull system so that work within ABC progressed only when the next step was ready for it.

While FIFO rules can help organize work between the various processes in the office, there is a big disconnect in the flow at the point of customer approval. What problems arise at this point? Is there any evidence of pushing the information forward that the team can eliminate with pull? In ABC's case, the team decided to create a prioritization of FIFO for the approvals received from the customer at the BOM/Purchase cell.

In the current state, the mapping team identified the quality-related issues associated with the bills-of-material that are a part of the job folder used throughout production. The team quickly realized that the job folder-related quality issues were a result of pushing—that is, printing out the job folder several weeks before production actually needed it. As a result, the job folder often did not reflect the most recent customer information.

The team decided to set up a pull system for the job folders going into production. When all materials were available to complete a job, production would trigger generation of the job folder. As a result, the job folder would contain the most recent information. Interestingly, ABC Design was already practicing an important application of pull concepts: They did not start any job in production until all required materials were available. In addition to the production "pull," the team also decided to create a FIFO prioritization for the customer approvals at the BOM/Purchase cell.

Leveling Work

Once the mapping team had a better understanding of interruptions, they were ready to ask the question, *How will the workload and/or activities be balanced?* That is, could they level the workload? Leveling work in an office environment has as much, if not more, benefit as leveling work on a production floor. At ABC, there is significant fluctuation in the processing times of both Enter Order/Generate Drawings and Generate BOM/Purchase. In many companies you can level these processing times by alternating jobs with high processing times (work content) with those with low processing times, thereby minimizing the impact on the organization. On the other hand, at ABC, there was an average of one order a day; some days they might not get an order, while on other days they might get three. In their case, they could possibly level the three orders by sorting them according to work content, and alternating big and small jobs. The result would be to level the needs of the cross-trained resources needed in the process and help reduce the variation in the lead times.

In ABC's first future state, however, they decided to take each order as it came in the door, and flex the workers to ensure that they could complete the processing in a short lead time. The cross-training kaizens already included these training requirements. ABC decided to manage the peaks and valleys of the processing time for each order using a management time frame of four hours. No more changes are required at this point for this first future state map.

Achieving ABC's Future State

The team's last question was: *What process improvements will be necessary to achieve the future state?* It will require implementing the process improvements we've discussed throughout this chapter, including:

- Replacing the existing order entry process with an online order entry process.

- Cross-training engineers to accept orders.

- Reorganizing the way engineering drawings are developed to allow parallel drawing work on large jobs.

- Automating the bill of material effort using the existing features in BizSys.

- Standardizing parts where possible to allow suppliers to build-to-stock.

- Developing blanket orders to reduce the work involved in the purchasing effort.

- Creating a BOM/Purchase cell capable of developing the BOM and initiating part purchasing in parallel with the customer approval process.

All of these improvements (kaizens) have been noted on ABC's future state map. By going through the future state design process, we've identified the key improvements necessary to drive the operations to achieve the business strategy: a competitive response to customer lead times. ABC can now organize and trigger cross-functional teams to develop the detail improvements necessary to see the future state to fruition.

As an aside, the natural inclination of many managers is to seek out technology improvements to achieve any and all improvements. After all, without improving these systems, how can you improve your current state? ABC's current state map had several systems issues that caused inefficiencies, including poor system integration and downtime in ACAD and BizSys systems. So why didn't ABC address these issues in its first future state design? ABC decided to focus on the fundamental work elements in the preproduction process, focusing on improving the effectiveness and efficiency of its work via improving policies, procedures, and the culture before addressing the technology systems that these fundamental work elements seemingly depend on. Therefore, as Figures 9-3A and 9-3B show, the mapping team purposely elected to show a future state with minimal technological solutions. Depending on the continuing needs of the enterprise to improve in the eyes of the (external) customer, ABC might eventually choose to address the system downtime or incorporate other technological systems, but this will happen after it has developed effective and more efficient processes.

ABC is now at a critical stage of developing a plan to implement the kaizens and sustain the gains for its future state. We'll discuss these issues in Chapter 10.

> *Team Exercise:* Figures 9-3A and 9-3B represents a future state on the preproduction process tasks of the enterprise. What might it look like if the mapping team focused on other processes, such as invoice and collect cash? Take a clean sheet of paper and draw a new alternative future state for these other tasks using the same questions discussed in this chapter.

Summing Up—Results of ABC's First Future State

ABC now has a new future state map, complete with anticipated performance improvements. How did ABC do in developing an operating strategy to achieve its business strategy of an eight-week (40-day) lead time? Table 9-1 outlines the results of the first future state map.

The difference between ABC's current and future state performance are impressive. ABC reduced the lead time to 37 business days, beating the goal of a 40-day (eight-week) lead time. In addition, 12 hours of processing time were eliminated and the first-pass yield rose from 44 percent to 91 percent.

Table 9-1. ABC Design Lead Time Improvement

	Enter Order	Generate Drawings	Generate BOM	Purchase	Pre-production lead time	Production lead time	Order lead time
Current state	4 days	5.5 days	1.5 days	18 days	44 days (including cust. approval)	5 days	49 days
Customer reqt. with time frame	4 days	1.5 days	1.5 days	18 days	40 days (including cust. approval)	5 days	45 days
Removing waste	1 day	1.5 days	1 day	15 days	33.5 days	5 days	38.5 days
Flowing work	0 days	1.5 days	0 days	15.5 days	32 days	5 days	37 days

ABC's focus on eliminating waste and improving flow has contributed significantly to its overall performance. Of course, the lead times represent the midpoint lead time of the individual process boxes. This puts pressure on finding ways in ABC's next future state design to reduce the maximum lead times and address the reliability in the office systems to hold the new lead times within the competitive range.

CHAPTER 10

Achieving the Future State

Value stream maps can be very useful tools in designing a new way of doing business, but they only represent the *beginning* of the lean journey. To embrace value stream management as a way of doing business, companies must implement the future state maps rapidly; that is, the organization must be committed to realizing the improvements. There are several critical success factors in achieving a lean transformation, but three are always at the top of the list:

1. Organizational leaders must understand and embrace lean concepts.
2. Value stream managers must have the authority and time to coordinate and facilitate the implementation.
3. Appropriate team members must develop detailed implementation plans for each kaizen, which are then used to manage the implementation.

There are many ways to go about prioritizing and implementing the changes required by the future state map. We offer a straightforward approach that has worked well in lean thinking companies.

Tie the Value Stream Design to the Company's Business Objectives

The lean journey is difficult, especially for those mature companies faced with an "anti-lean" culture of anchor-dragging managers who are antagonistic to the lean way. This makes it even more imperative for those trained and committed in lean thinking to stay "on message" in training and turning early adopters into true believers, who in turn will help win over the more cautious employees. This means management must focus on making sure the company's operating strategy (i.e., its future state map) reflects its business plan (i.e., the company's strategy), and they must support complementary lean choices in the future state design.

In ABC's case, the business objective was to create a competitive lead time of eight weeks for designing and producing custom-ordered products to maintain and improve sales. As a result, they focused their value stream design to reduce this lead time. However, time is not the only element in maintaining and improving sales. If for instance, ABC improved their lead time to match or better their competition but their cost remained high, then they would need to focus their value stream design on understanding and reducing this cost.

Break the Work Plan into Loops

When you examine all the kaizens necessary to implement ABC's future state, there is a lot of work to do! The best approach is for the mapping team to divide this work into logical elements, known as loops, and focus on the implementation effort within each loop. The value stream manager is then responsible for overseeing each of the loops, which he and the mapping team can also sequence and prioritize during implementation.

Loops typically represent areas of flow. Shop floor maps usually document three to five loops. The loop concept is more difficult to identify in the office since many unnecessary handoffs (i.e., areas of flow) probably still exist in the initial future state map. As a company moves forward with additional future state maps, it will become easier to limit loops to individual areas of flow. However, the mapping team can employ a similar thought process to establish groups of flow that tie together similar themes. Figures 10-1A and 10-1B show that there are two loops prior to ABC's production. The order entry loop comprises all the work necessary to document and communicate the order information to the customer. The post-approval loop comprises all the work necessary to translate customer needs into available parts to begin fabrication on the shop floor.

Prioritize Loop Implementation

While dividing the future state map into loops helps in organizing and managing the implementation, the team must still deal with several loops and multiple kaizens within each loop. These activities must therefore be prioritized to manage implementation resources effectively.

Let's prioritize ABC's implementation loops. We have a post-approval loop and an order entry loop. Which loop appears to be the most important to address? Within the production (raw material-to-customer) value stream organizations typically choose what is referred to as a pacemaker loop. This is usually the furthest downstream loop in the facility. For ABC we don't have that option since it already addressed this value stream before taking an enterprise perspective. Another way to prioritize loops is to look at the organization's strategic plan and determine which loop has the largest impact on the cost, service, and quality of the enterprise products as seen by the customer. As we think through ABC's loops, it appears that the 11-day reduction in lead time within the order entry loop might be the place to start. The lead time reduction will be impressive to customers since they will see drawings ready for their approval in just 1.5 days. What a strong selling point!

To prioritize kaizens within loops and minimize implementation resources, we use the following common sense approach.

- Eliminate non-value-added tasks that don't require new information technology efforts.

- Simplify the remaining steps that require minimal information technology support (e.g., minimizing transactions entering the value stream).

- Implement flow of transactions or paperwork: process one, move one (e.g., improve office layout, cross-training, cell implementation).

- Implement the solutions requiring significant information technology support.

Using this prioritization helps the mapping team focus on simplifying the functions and eliminating waste before using and/or investing in technology, which extends the value stream's productivity. We can't know all the details that drove ABC's decisions, but we can offer a reasonable prioritization within each loop.

Order entry Loop

While it's possible to argue how to prioritize based on each particular value stream, ABC wanted its first priority to be an online order entry function because it would eliminate non-value-added work (discrepancy forms) and smooth the input of information so orders didn't get hung up waiting for complete and accurate information from sales. This seemed to be a good place to begin since the order entry personnel were knowledgeable in BizSys and could work through the bugs more readily than the engineers. The engineers could be cross-trained later on to get up to speed.

The second priority within this loop was redesigning the drawing activity to allow engineers to share work on large drawings. This prioritization made sense because the engineers could continue to focus on their work while ABC implemented the new order entry function.

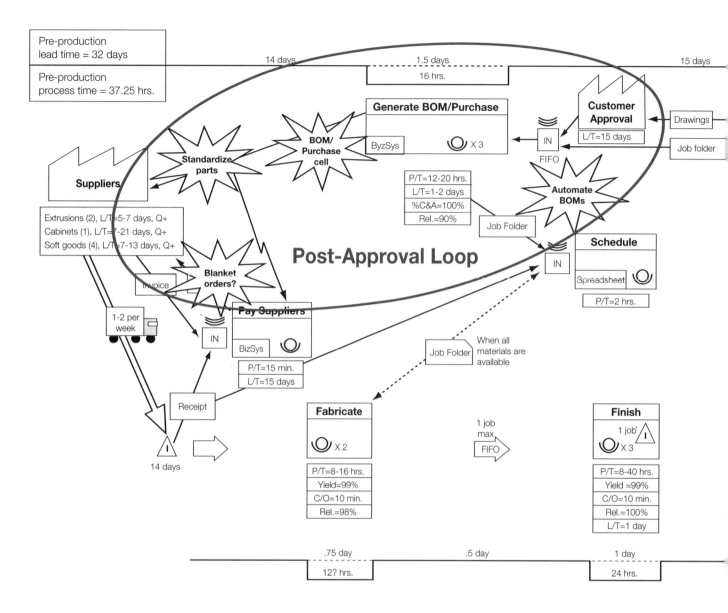

Figure 10-1A. Post-Approval Loop

The third priority was to cross-train the engineers. Because cross-training involves new tools and responsibilities, it's best to use the first two kaizens to simplify the tasks and develop as much standardized work as possible for a smooth transition to the new changes.

In summary, the overall objectives of the order entry loop include:

- Kaizen 1: Develop online order entry to reduce lead time and improve the quality of the incoming information.

- Kaizen 2: Redesign the work content to enable splitting drawings among several engineers to reduce drawing lead time.

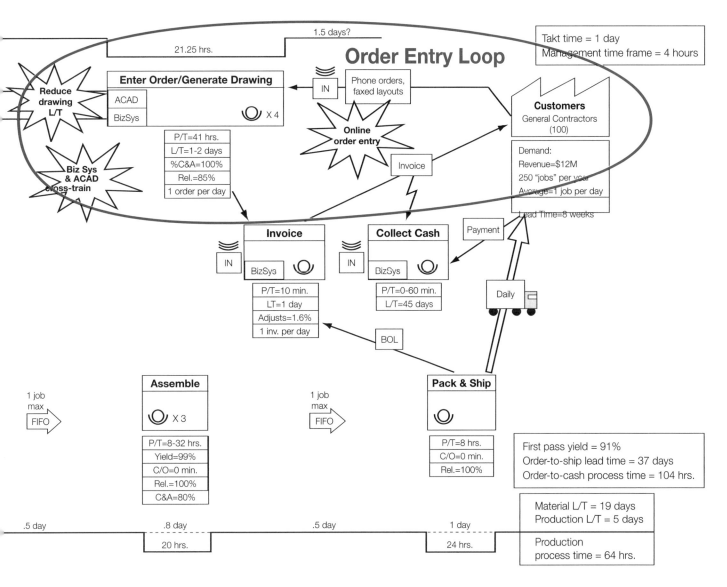

Figure 10-1B. Order Entry Loop

- Kaizen 3: Cross-train two additional engineers in ACAD and all four engineers to enter orders from the field.

The goals within the loop include:

- Only 1.5 days of lead time to complete drawings for customer approval.

- 100 percent C&A information on each order being entered.

- Four engineers supporting order entry and drawing generation.

- Four-hour intervals between reviews of work to maintain a 1.5-day turn-around time to the customer.

Post-Approval Loop

ABC believed that the basis of a successful post approval loop was developing a higher level of standardized parts because it would make it easier to generate a BOM and purchase parts. Once it achieved a high level of standardization, it would be easier to develop blanket orders that would further minimize the purchasing interface and work content in the future work cell. In addition, ABC thought that the BOM automation should take place prior to the development of the cell because it would reduce the work content associated with the cell and ensure a staffing level of three people.

If ABC had different resources associated with implementing the blanket orders and automate BOMs kaizens, these kaizens could take place in parallel without any problem. If they had resource constraints, then they would choose one kaizen over the other. Finally, once they eliminate the work content from the BOM and purchasing tasks, it would make sense to develop the BOM/purchase cell.

In summary, the overall objectives of the post-approval loop include:

- Kaizen 1: Standardize parts to minimize the effort for a blanket purchase order and reduce the work content associated with purchasing as well as reduce the lead time of purchased parts from suppliers.

- Kaizen 2: Create blanket purchase orders to reduce the purchasing work content and reduce the lead time of purchased parts from suppliers.

- Kaizen 3: Automate the BOM process to reduce the work content of BOM generation, free up people to assist with drawings, and increase the quality of the part information sent to purchasing.

- Kaizen 4: Create a cell to develop the BOM and purchase parts for manufacturing.

The goals within the loop include:

- Vendor lead times of 7 to 21 days.

- No incremental lead time associated with BOM generation and purchasing.

- 100 percent C&A information sent to the vendors.

- Processing time of 12–20 hours to create a BOM and purchase parts.

- Three people operating the BOM/Purchase cell.

- Four-hour intervals between reviews of the cell work to maintain a "zero" lead time to get purchase information to the suppliers.

Create a Work Plan and Cross-Functional Implementation Teams

After all the hard work involved in designing a new value stream, the downfall of most companies is not putting enough energy into creating and implementing an effective work plan. ABC prepared for this crucial stage by defining the future state implementation loops and prioritizing the work within each loop. These plans included:

- What has to be done (look at the kaizens).

- How the company will measure success (look at the new data in the data box).

- Who will be involved in completing each kaizen (both team leaders and cross-functional team members).

- When each kaizen will begin and end and when checkpoints will be reviewed by management.

The actual plan document looks like a Gantt chart and is used by the value stream manager and the management team to track the progress of the effort. We've created a future state plan for ABC as an example (see Figure 10-2).

Process Improvement	Goal(s)	Month											
		1	2	3	4	5	6	7	8	9	10	11	12
Order-Entry Loop													
Online order entry (including checklist)	100% C&A L/T = 1 day	→											
Reduce drawing L/T (smaller batches, parallel processing)	L/T = 1–2 days			→									
BizSys & ACAD cross-training	100% cross trained	→											
Post-Approval Loop													
BOM/purchase cell, develop BOM in parallel to customer approval	L/T = 1/2 day						→						
Automate bill of materials (BOM) using BizSys capabilities	100% C&A P/T = 8–16 hours L/T = 1 day						→						
Standardize parts, establish blanket	Supplier L/T = 7–21 days							→					

Value Stream Manager: _____

Team Members: _____

_____

Review Dates _____

Figure 10-2. Implementation Work Plan

Mapping Tip: Consider having information technology personnel represented in many kaizens so they can learn to see the flow of the information, which will help in guiding future IT designs.

Lean Note: The mapping team uses kaizens on the value stream map to indicate areas of special concern. In the implementation stage, the appropriate team member usually runs a kaizen workshop to implement a set of techniques and processes as required by the future state. Typically, kaizens use Deming's plan-do-check-act (PDCA) cycle, as well as documentation, standardization, visual management, and time management to develop strategies to ensure long-lasting improvement. It is also a way to help educate employees in lean thinking via a train-do focus.

Now comes the hard part: getting each of the new implementation teams together to hash out the details concerning each kaizen. The mapping team only provided a brief description of each kaizen on the future state plan. The cross-functional team must decide the individual steps necessary to achieve this plan, with subsets of who, what, how, and when for each of these individual steps. This is a critical success factor of implementing future states. If the cross-functional team doesn't approach an individual kaizen quickly as a team effort, the work will typically fall to the person in charge who will do it by the seat of his or her pants without effective input from the organization. As a result, the company will rarely achieve the desired goal.

Once the future state design and a detailed work plan are in place, it's time to begin implementation. To ensure success, top management should review this plan on a regular basis—maybe three or four times within the duration of each future state implementation.

Enabling Value Stream Management

Value stream management encourages flexibility in meeting market needs through:

- Growth with improved margins.

- Growth with minimal capital.

- Growth without additional personnel.

A simple but effective way for management to support value stream management is to require value stream maps for every request for additional capital and/or people. Management meetings could begin with a discussion on the various value streams, determine which requests are valid, and begin dealing with company issues within the context of the newly identified value streams. Many requests might need a lean evaluation of the value stream needs and flexible ways to use existing resources.

Management can also support value stream management in using lean metrics to determine the effectiveness of the value streams. What metrics should you use? Policy deployment can provide some guidelines, but a good source is using the metrics the mapping team has identified on the value stream maps, such as process time, % C&A, lead time, etc. These process-level metrics ultimately define the cost, service, and quality of the value stream.

Organization by value streams can also support value stream management. It may be possible to break the traditional centralized support mode of preproduction into several small, effective support groups, each dedicated to a specific product family. We aren't suggesting that this should be a company's unexamined goal, but an option to think through as it assesses its value streams with an enterprise perspective. The result of such an effort would be an extension of the focused factory within the office.

Finally, nothing encourages a corporation to support a new way of thinking about business than the acceptance of the new philosophy by its financial organization. Finance department support can begin by establishing lean metrics and links to existing metrics that report up the organizational ladder throughout the company. Finance can also support value stream management by focusing on more important issues than the traditional metrics in a lean transformation. This would include determining the true cost of a value stream and projecting how the balance sheet and P&L statement will change as the company implements its future states. A major barrier to this is the company's reliance on the traditional costing of indirect and administrative costs based on burden absorption. While this type of allocation is convenient for reporting purposes, it does nothing to assist the organization in managing its overhead in an effective manner. Determining the actual costs of the administrative and indirect support in value streams challenges this profound impact on the current understanding of product costs, and can be a great way to support the challenges of value stream management.

In the end, all that companies are trying to do is increase the value of the organization as perceived by the market. Incorporating a lean strategy, within the context of value stream management, is an effective and efficient way to achieve this goal. It is management's responsibility to lead the lean transformation of the enterprise through support of value stream implementations, and by embracing and demonstrating lean thinking in all areas of the organization. It is our sincere hope that this workbook has provided your company with the necessary guidelines, maps, value stream processes, and lean terminology to help you in this task. The organization's ultimate success rests directly on management's commitment to creating the culture and climate capable of sustaining a lean enterprise.

APPENDIX

ABC Order Entry/Drawing Case Study— Cross-Functional Level Mapping

Now that the ABC management has understood its enterprise from a site-level perspective, it's time for them to drill down through their existing map to understand how to design their improvements at a cross-functional level. Remember, there are four levels of value stream mapping: across companies, site/multisite, cross-functional, and process. The site-level map now becomes the framework for the detailed efforts in cross-functional and process-level mapping. That is, the future states of any additional supporting maps should support the overall goal of the site-level map in structure, function, and performance.

> *Mapping Note:* Some companies begin mapping at the cross-functional level (as opposed to a site level) for the office support areas, once they have already value stream mapped and implemented lean thinking on the production floor. If you are comfortable knowing where to expand your lean effort, use this approach to develop your current and future state maps, and use the same future state questions discussed in Chapters 8 and 9 regarding ABC's future state.

One of the main areas of redesign in ABC's enterprise future state map was the transformation of both order entry and drawing generation (the order entry loop). The site-level map designed this as a combined function, with a different way to enter orders and schedule drawings. We'll use this area to demonstrate how ABC can drill down to a cross-functional-level redesign.

> *Team Exercise:* Your team may want to try its own hand at mapping the order entry loop. They can use the maps in this appendix as a reference. How you visualize a process may be slightly different from how ABC visualized the same process.

Current State Map for Order Entry and Drawing

ABC Design assembled a cross-functional team of order entry and engineering management (plus a few functional experts) to work on combining order entry and drawing. They walked the flow to document the following current state for customer requirements, work processes, and process information:

Customer Requirements

- One order per day, with a wide range of size and complexity.

- Lead time (of this loop) averaging 1.5 days (based on the site-level future state map).

Work Processes

- As documented in the enterprise map, field sales sends orders into ABC with plans and spec sheets. Order entry personnel then review these orders for complete and accurate information and enter them into the BizSys system.

- If the order is lacking information, it is marked as a *preliminary order* in the system and order entry personnel request additional information by phone from the salesperson responsible for the order.

- The salesperson forwards the additional information by phone and mail to order entry, where it is reviewed again and finalized in BizSys. At this point, order entry makes a call to the finance department for a credit check. If the credit is good, customer service prints the order and places it in a job folder for engineering, along with the plans and spec sheet.

- The job folder is reviewed by the engineering manager for accuracy and then scheduled for work between the two engineers.

- Once the assigned engineer selects the packet to work on, it is researched to identify any unusual requests in design: forms, fabrics, or physical layout.

- The engineer then creates a two-dimensional CAD drawing.

- Once the drawing is complete, another engineer checks the work for accuracy and puts it aside for a formal engineering review and sign-off by the engineering and sales managers.

- Once the drawings are signed-off by sales and engineering, the databases are updated and the drawings distributed to sales and the customer.

(Note: The handoff to the BOM Process in our case study is not depicted on our map.)

Process Information

The process data attributes can differ from those chosen for the site-level map, since participants may have a better understanding for defining cost, service, and quality indicators. For this case study, the data attributes remain the same as those used in the site-level map.

- **Review and Enter Order:**

  Process Time: 10 – 20 minutes

  Lead Time: 4 hours

  % C&A: 60%

  Reliability: 95%

  IT Tool: BizSys

  Processing Priority: First-In, First-Out

- **Request Information:**

  Process Time: 10 minutes

  Lead Time: 1 – 6 days

  Processing Priority: Due Date

- **Finalize and Print Order:**

  Process Time: 10 – 30 minutes

  Lead Time: 4 – 8 hours

  % C&A: 99%

  % Credit hold: 1%

  Reliability: 95%

  IT Tool: BizSys

  Processing Priority: Due Date

- **Review and Schedule Order:**

  Process Time: 1– 10 minutes

  Lead Time: 4 - 8 hours

  % C&A: 95%

  Processing Priority: Size of Job

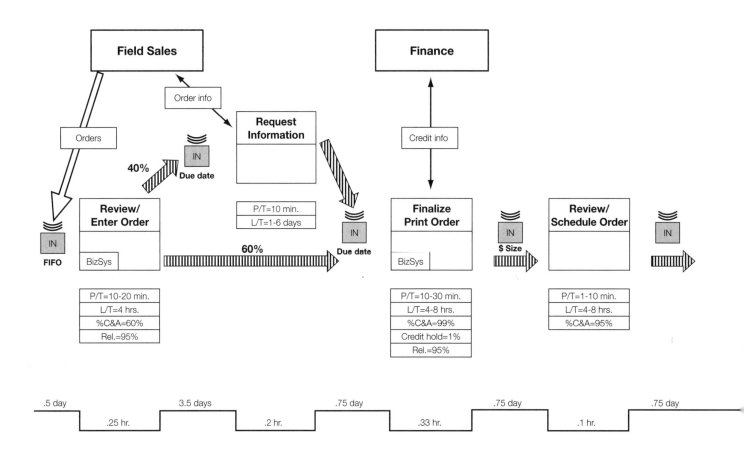

Figure A-1. Order Entry/Drawing Current State

- **Research Order:**
  Process Time: 0 – 60 minutes
  Lead Time: 4 – 8 hours

- **Create Drawing:**
  Process Time: .5 – 35 hours
  Lead Time: .5 – 7 days
  Reliability: 90%
  IT Tool: ACAD
  Processing Priority: First-In, First-Out

- **Check Drawing:**
  Process Time: .5 – 4 hours
  Lead Time: .5 – 12 hours

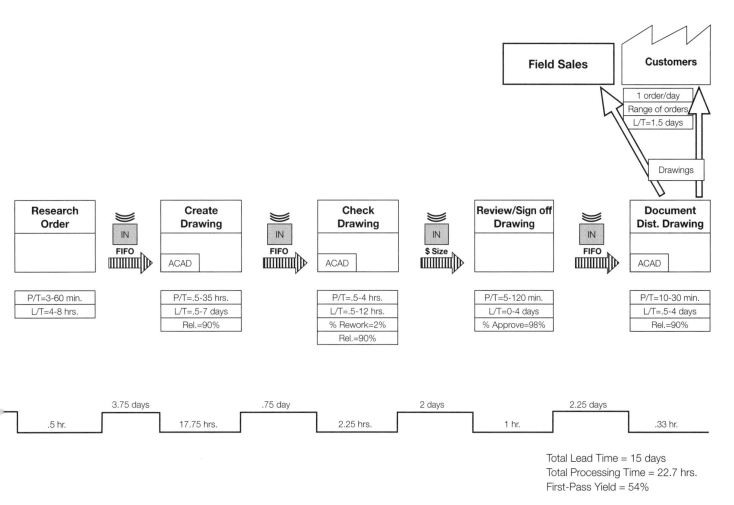

Figure A-2. Order Entry/Drawing Current State, (*continued*)

Reliability: 90%

% Rework: 2%

IT Tool: ACAD

Processing Priority: First-In, First-Out

- **Review Drawing and Sign Off:**

  Process Time = 5 – 120 minutes

  Lead Time: 0 – 4 days

  % Approved: 98%

  Processing Priority: Size of Job

- **Document and Distribute Drawing:**

  Processing Time: 10 – 30 minutes

  Lead Time: .5 – 4 days

IT Tool: ACAD

Reliability: 90%

Processing Priority: First-In, First-Out

The team put all this together and created Figures A-1 and A-2.

Future State Map Discussion

Remember, there is more than one solution in creating a future state to support the organization's strategy. This discussion demonstrates one that supports the enterprise future state framework of:

- Online order entry within engineering.

- Split drawings and "floating" support.

Each of these is discussed in the following sections.

Online Order Entry: Future States One and Two

ABC management wanted to enter orders within engineering. Based on the current state map, they redesigned the flow of work in order entry before handing this responsibility over to engineering. After all, management designed this piece of the enterprise future state by asking, "Where do we flow?" To flow the work, the future state must combine the job elements of:

- Review and Enter Order.

- Request Information.

- Finalize and Print Order.

- Review and Schedule Order.

To accommodate flow in this area, the site-level future state map charged ABC with creating an online order entry process. Once the current state map visualized the process (Figures A-1 and A-2), management felt it could facilitate this concept by removing the disconnect of incomplete orders. By developing standards (or standardized work) for creating an order in the field, ABC could eliminate the rework embedded in this task. Management chose to develop a sales checklist with the help of the sales, order entry, and engineering departments. The checklist would guide the sales force to develop complete and accurate information and specifications for each order.

Once ABC incorporated standardized work into the process and initiated the phone and fax features to enter orders, it was possible to enter, finalize, and print orders all at once, which created flow. (Note: it's also possible to embed the standard of phoning in the order and faxing the layout in this checklist,

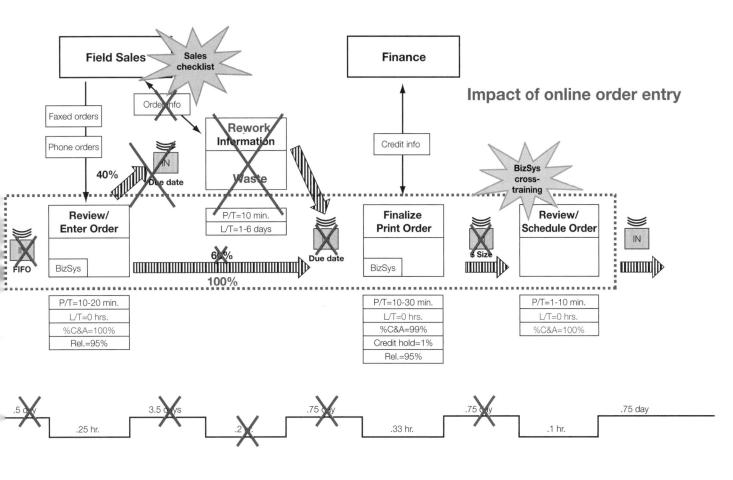

Figure A-3. Order Entry/Drawing Future State 1

complete with phone numbers!) At this point, the process could be handed over to the engineers to enter the orders. However, management also chose to stretch this process into the scheduling of the work, enabling the engineer entering the order to automatically schedule the drawing work.

Figure A-3, Order Entry/Drawing Future State 1, represents the changes discussed so far. It demonstrates the impact of taking orders as they come in, with the various queues eliminated along with the process time associated with the rework waste of requesting more order information. In order to achieve this future state, the team identified two distinct kaizens: developing a sales checklist and cross-training the engineers to enable them to enter order information in BizSys.

However, ABC also realized that flow associated with order entry was still hampered by the credit check function: They couldn't move an order forward without first checking a customer's credit situation! Figure A-4, Order

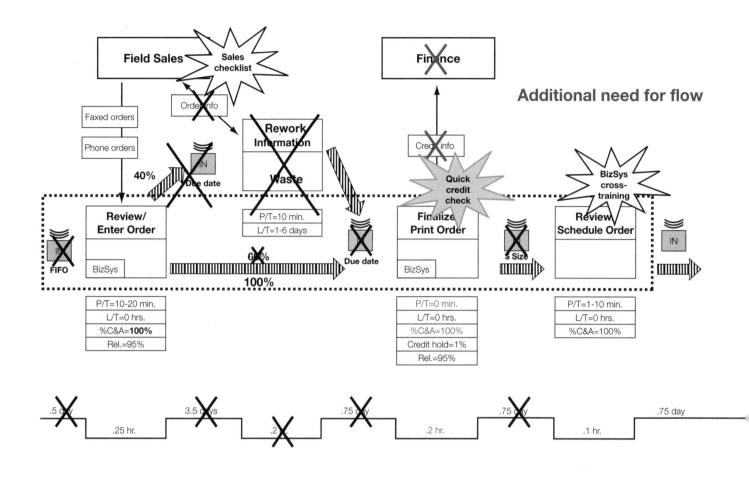

Figure A-4. Order Entry/Drawing Future State 2

Entry/Drawing Future State 2, goes a step further and eliminates this financial handoff by adding a quick credit check kaizen to the map, reducing the process time to a projected 10 minutes. There are several ways to accomplish this "quality at the source" issue (e.g., online credit ratings or a regularly updated list of good or bad companies). It will be up to the kaizen team to make the best choice for creating a future state that improves the overall process (not just the financial process).

Split Drawing and Floating Support: Future States 3 and 4

In this final area in the order entry loop the team had to determine how to use several engineers to process pieces of a design in parallel to ensure a consistent, quick response time for drawings sent to customers for approval. The ABC Order Entry/Drawing Current State map (Figures A-1 and A-2) shows five more tasks the team needed to address:

1. Research Order.
2. Create Drawing.
3. Check Drawing.
4. Review and Sign off Drawing.
5. Document and Distribute Drawing.

To achieve flow, ABC zeroed in on the final two drawing steps: review and sign off and document and distribute. There was difficulty getting everyone together in a timely fashion to review the drawings. The average waiting period to schedule a review meeting was two days. In addition, for no apparent reason, there were 1.75 days of queue in between these two steps. The team decided to combine these steps as well as address the waiting waste in setting up the review meetings. By creatively manipulating ABC's current computer systems, the team found a way to enable online reviews by the necessary parties, and to distribute the drawings automatically to the next step in the process when a person completed a review. (In their case, it was the customer and sales.)

While this process appeared to be solid, there were times that the right people weren't available to sign off on the review, still necessitating a long review turnaround. After further discussions, ABC elected to set up a simple system that communicated who was responsible for approving drawings each day based on who was available either in the office or online. Furthermore, the designated people were required to check for drawings every two hours, and to review/approve all drawings in the queue. While this appears to be cumbersome on the surface, this procedure reinforces many lean features:

- *Small batch sizes.* ABC only has to review two hours of work at any time, and ABC estimates that the required review time will be no more than 20 minutes. This means that a drawing for a desk area can be reviewed even while the shelving drawing is being worked on.

- *Flow.* Small batches are distributed immediately after the review, eliminating 1.75 days of lead time and 20 minutes of processing time.

- *Team concepts, cross-training, and standardized work.* Several more people will be responsible for reviewing drawings in the event that the regular checkers are not available. This will necessitate standard ways to review drawings for all concerned.

With the review effort streamlined, ABC also looked at the actual creation and checking of the drawings. It wanted to replicate the same rigorous two-hour cadence of the review upstream. By checking available drawings every two hours, ABC could move the documents at the same cadence governing the reviewers, ensuring a smoother flow of small batches of paperwork. To accomplish this, ABC would have to designate and cross-train its checkers (remember, there are now four engineers assigned to this area) with clear communication as to who was responsible for this task each day. (Note: The site-level future state stipulated a management time frame of four hours. When the team dug deeper into the cross-functional future state, they were comfortable with a more aggressive management time frame, which still conforms to the enterprise needs.)

Another facet of organizing the work in this process was how ABC needed to prioritize the work between each area of flow. In the current state, there was a wide range of work prioritizations, such as size of the job, due date, and FIFO. ABC elected to emphasize a consistent, quick turnaround by establishing a FIFO lane with only two hours of work in it. In this manner, each job moved ahead at the same rate. Combined with the frequent review, each job also moved ahead quickly!

With the FIFO sized at two hours, it also enabled the upstream processes to avoid overproducing. If the lane was full, ABC didn't process any more work. Instead, it could find out what was causing the lane to be full and then deploy resources (i.e., people) to help balance the workload. Figure A-5 shows the new ideas and expected performances for Order Entry/Drawing Future State 3.

The final area ABC looked at was the creation of drawings. This might be the largest creative challenge within ABC Design: How to divide the work into smaller elements and balance the workload to respond to an order quickly. With the engineers now accepting the orders, ABC should be able to divide the drawing work into smaller increments. While no order could be divided perfectly into equal work parts, ABC could break down the work elements into logical chunks, such as shelves versus cabinets, that would help organize the work into small batches.

ABC decided to tackle all these issues by the trigger (signal) used to begin the drawings once they took an order from a customer. In addition, once the drawing order was assigned to the engineer, they believed it was possible to research the drawing. The engineer would then immediately begin the drawing after the research, creating flow between two process tasks in the current state. And, if ABC did a better job of standardizing parts and organizing the research effort, it could simplify the research so it would require less time. In addition, if ABC had smaller amounts of work generated in a single drawing session, it would take less time to check these drawings. ABC estimated that they could break the work up into units of about four hours and check these drawings in about 30 minutes.

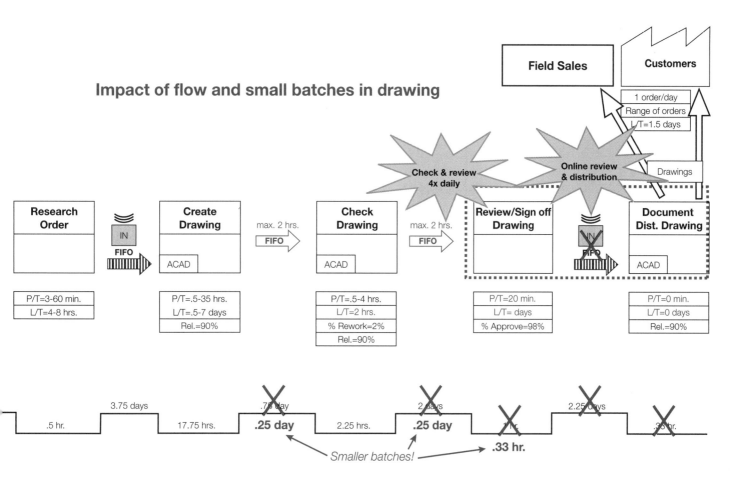

Figure A-5. Order Entry/Drawing Future State 3

One way ABC could schedule or trigger work is by using a schedule board in engineering. This board could be anything from a whiteboard to a computer spreadsheet. The engineer taking each order could populate the schedule board with relatively small amounts of drawing work. The engineer could split up the order and move it into open slots on the schedule. If ABC limited the schedule board to allow no more than one day of backlog, it could see when the two primary engineers were scheduled to capacity and begin to schedule one or two other engineers. (Remember, two engineers are now available from the BOM process). This scheduling tool would provide a way to visually balance the resources and predict the lead time for specific jobs.

Figure A-6, Order Entry/Drawing Future State 4, shows the changes necessary to accommodate the splitting up of drawings and the balancing of work within the check drawing process.

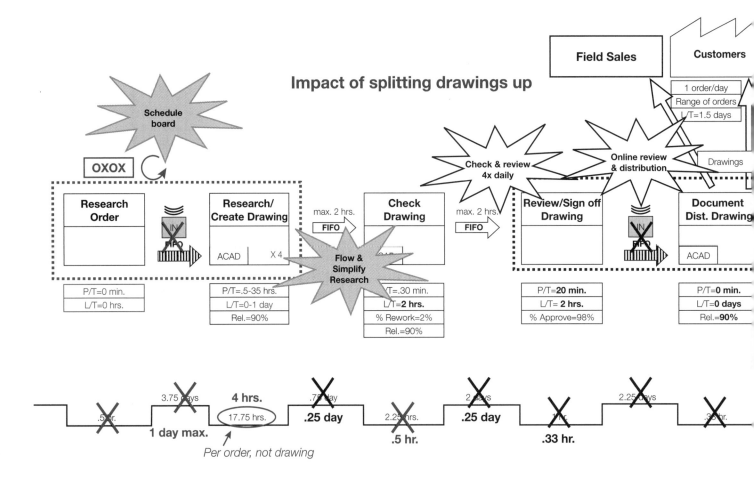

Figure A-6. Order Entry/Drawing Future State 4

Putting It Together: Future State 5

Finally, ABC combined all of the details of the future state into Figure A-7, Order Entry/Drawing Future State 5. This map reflects all of the process and performance changes ABC believed it was capable of achieving in a six-month time frame (minus the kaizens, which they placed in the detailed work plan). By using a variety of lean concepts and tools to improve the cost, service, and speed of the order entry loop of the enterprise, ABC improved lead time by 89 percent, processing time by 16 percent and process quality by 76 percent.

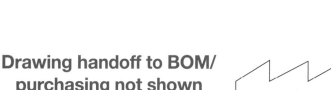

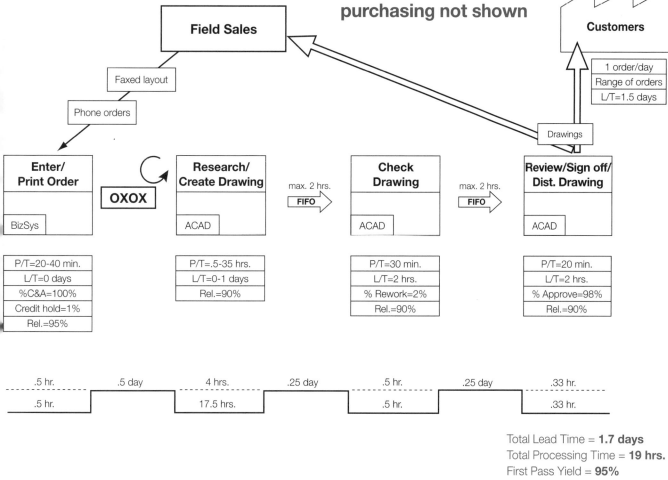

Figure A-7. Order Entry/Drawing Future State 5

However, even with these value stream improvements, the team has not met the initial requirement of delivering the drawing to the customer in 1.5 days. Since the future state lead time is "close" (at 1.7 days), ABC management has a choice: accept the 1.7 days or ask the team for additional improvements, such as eliminating the Review/Signoff with Sales (note high approval levels) and distributing drawings from the Check Drawing step.

ABC Design

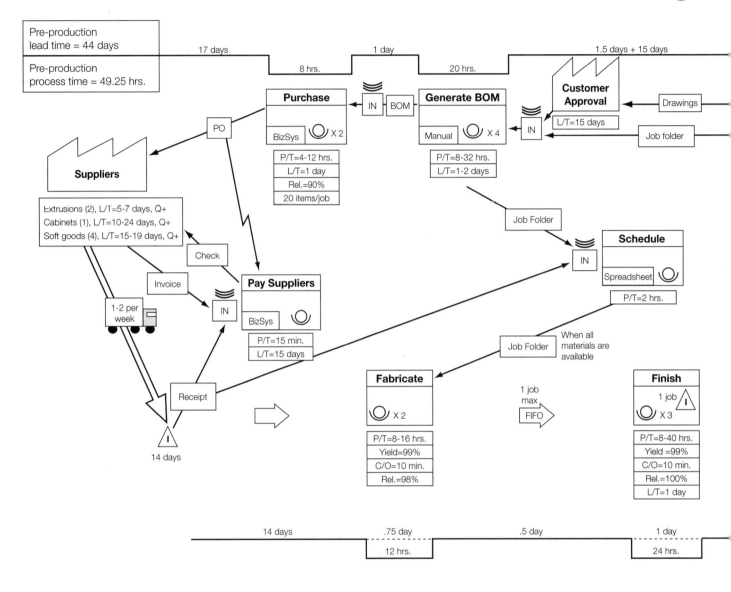

Pre-production
lead time = 44 days

Pre-production
process time = 49.25 hrs.

17 days   1 day   1.5 days + 15 days

8 hrs.   20 hrs.

Purchase   IN   BOM   **Generate BOM**   **Customer Approval**   Drawings

BizSys X 2   Manual X 4   L/T=15 days   Job folder

P/T=4-12 hrs.   P/T=8-32 hrs.
L/T=1 day   L/T=1-2 days
Rel.=90%
20 items/job

PO

Suppliers

Extrusions (2), L/T=5-7 days, Q+
Cabinets (1), L/T=10-24 days, Q+
Soft goods (4), L/T=15-19 days, Q+

Job Folder

Check   **Schedule**

IN

Invoice   Spreadsheet

1-2 per
week   IN   **Pay Suppliers**   P/T=2 hrs.

BizSys

P/T=15 min.   When all
L/T=15 days   materials are
available

Job Folder

Receipt   **Fabricate**   1 job   **Finish**
max
X 2   FIFO   1 job X 3

14 days   P/T=8-16 hrs.   P/T=8-40 hrs.
Yield=99%   Yield =99%
C/O=10 min.   C/O=10 min.
Rel.=98%   Rel.=100%
L/T=1 day

14 days   .75 day   .5 day   1 day

12 hrs.   24 hrs.

Current State Map

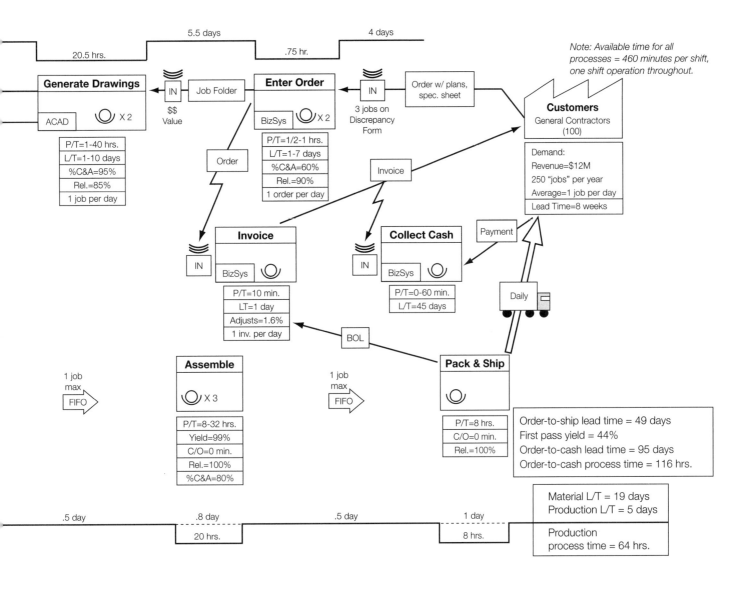

Generate Drawings
ACAD ⊙ X 2
P/T=1-40 hrs.
L/T=1-10 days
%C&A=95%
Rel.=85%
1 job per day

5.5 days
20.5 hrs.

IN
Job Folder
$$
Value

Enter Order
BizSys ⊙ X 2
P/T=1/2-1 hrs.
L/T=1-7 days
%C&A=60%
Rel.=90%
1 order per day

4 days
.75 hr.

IN
3 jobs on
Discrepancy
Form

Order w/ plans,
spec. sheet

Customers
General Contractors
(100)
Demand:
Revenue=$12M
250 "jobs" per year
Average=1 job per day
Lead Time=8 weeks

Note: Available time for all
processes = 460 minutes per shift,
one shift operation throughout.

Order

Invoice

Invoice
BizSys ⊙
P/T=10 min.
LT=1 day
Adjusts=1.6%
1 inv. per day

IN

Collect Cash
BizSys ⊙
P/T=0-60 min.
L/T=45 days

IN

Payment

Daily

BOL

Assemble
⊙ X 3
P/T=8-32 hrs.
Yield=99%
C/O=0 min.
Rel.=100%
%C&A=80%

1 job
max
FIFO

Pack & Ship
⊙
P/T=8 hrs.
C/O=0 min.
Rel.=100%

1 job
max
FIFO

Order-to-ship lead time = 49 days
First pass yield = 44%
Order-to-cash lead time = 95 days
Order-to-cash process time = 116 hrs.

Material L/T = 19 days
Production L/T = 5 days

Production
process time = 64 hrs.

.5 day   .8 day   .5 day   1 day
                20 hrs.   8 hrs.

ABC Design

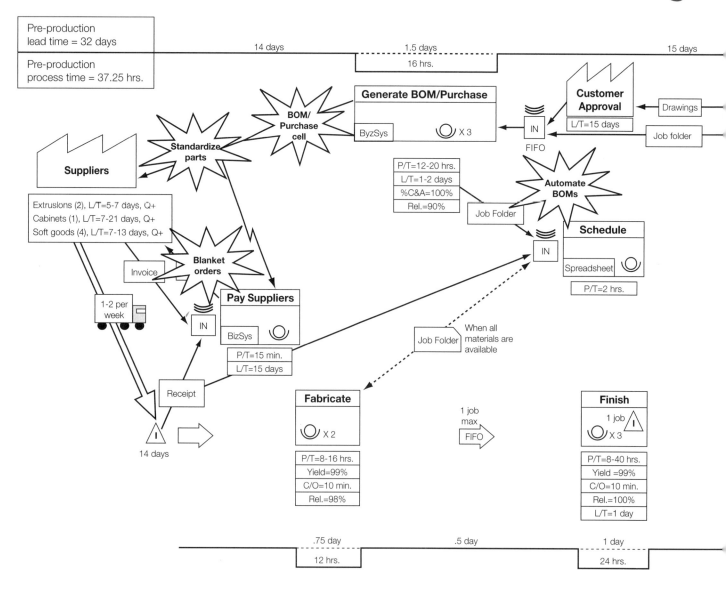

Pre-production
lead time = 32 days

Pre-production
process time = 37.25 hrs.

14 days   1.5 days   15 days
                 16 hrs.

Generate BOM/Purchase

BOM/
Purchase
cell

ByzSys   X 3

Customer Approval

Drawings

IN
FIFO

L/T=15 days

Job folder

Suppliers

Standardize parts

Extrusions (2), L/T=5-7 days, Q+
Cabinets (1), L/T=7-21 days, Q+
Soft goods (4), L/T=7-13 days, Q+

P/T=12-20 hrs.
L/T=1-2 days
%C&A=100%
Rel.=90%

Automate BOMs

Job Folder

IN

Schedule

Spreadsheet

P/T=2 hrs.

Invoice

Blanket orders

1-2 per week

IN

Pay Suppliers

BizSys

P/T=15 min.
L/T=15 days

Job Folder

When all
materials are
available

Receipt

14 days

Fabricate

X 2

P/T=8-16 hrs.
Yield=99%
C/O=10 min.
Rel.=98%

1 job
max

FIFO

Finish

1 job

X 3

P/T=8-40 hrs.
Yield =99%
C/O=10 min.
Rel.=100%
L/T=1 day

.75 day   .5 day   1 day
12 hrs.   24 hrs.

Future State Map

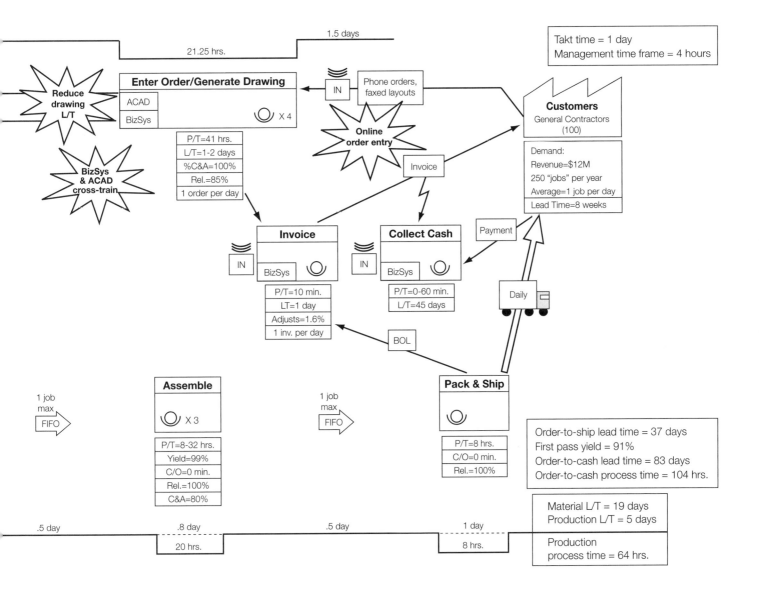

Enter Order/Generate Drawing
- ACAD
- BizSys
- X 4

P/T=41 hrs.
L/T=1-2 days
%C&A=100%
Rel.=85%
1 order per day

1.5 days

21.25 hrs.

Reduce drawing L/T

BizSys & ACAD cross-train

IN — Phone orders, faxed layouts

Online order entry

Invoice

Takt time = 1 day
Management time frame = 4 hours

Customers
General Contractors (100)

Demand:
Revenue=$12M
250 "jobs" per year
Average=1 job per day
Lead Time=8 weeks

Invoice
IN | BizSys
P/T=10 min.
LT=1 day
Adjusts=1.6%
1 inv. per day

Collect Cash
IN | BizSys
P/T=0-60 min.
L/T=45 days

Payment

Daily

BOL

Assemble
X 3
P/T=8-32 hrs.
Yield=99%
C/O=0 min.
Rel.=100%
C&A=80%

1 job max — FIFO

1 job max — FIFO

Pack & Ship
P/T=8 hrs.
C/O=0 min.
Rel.=100%

Order-to-ship lead time = 37 days
First pass yield = 91%
Order-to-cash lead time = 83 days
Order-to-cash process time = 104 hrs.

Material L/T = 19 days
Production L/T = 5 days

Production process time = 64 hrs.

.5 day

.8 day — 20 hrs.

.5 day

1 day — 8 hrs.

INDEX

ABOUT THE AUTHORS

James "Beau" Keyte

Beau Keyte is the founder of Branson, Inc., a management consulting company focused on the application of lean manufacturing strategies and techniques. Beau began his lean consulting career in the mid-'80s at the Ford Motor Company. He has clients in a wide variety of industries such as automotive, pharmaceutical, chemical, health care, financial services, consumer goods, industrial goods, and transportation. He has focused his implementation efforts on and off the shop floor and has successfully adapted many of the lean techniques to the front office since 1992. Beau has also successfully tied lean initiatives to the bottom line through the application of lean cost management techniques.

In addition to assisting companies in implementing lean strategies, Beau also trains manufacturers in a variety of public and private settings. He is currently a faculty member and instructor for the lean manufacturing curriculums at the Lean Enterprise Institute, Ford Motor Company, the University of Michigan, Ohio State University, and the National Institute of Standards and Technology (NIST), where he has assisted in the development and implementation of a consistent training program for use within small- and medium-sized manufacturers. Beau received a Bachelor of Science in Engineering and a Masters in Business Administration from the University of Michigan.

www.bransoninc.com

Drew A. Locher

Drew is currently Managing Director for Change Management Associates (CMA). CMA provides lean enterprise consulting and organizational development services to industrial and service organizations representing a wide variety of industries including health care, transportation, distribution, education, financial services, and manufacturing. Drew first became involved in the development and delivery of innovative business improvement programs while working for General Electric in the 1980s. In 1990, Drew left GE to form CMA. Since then, he has utilized his diverse experience to help develop creative solutions for the companies with whom CMA works, in order to improve their business performance.

Drew received a Bachelor of Science degree from the University of Delaware in Mechanical Engineering, as well as a Master of Science degree from Drexel University in Electrical and Computer Engineering. He has also received a Master of Business Administration from Cornell University. He is a member of the American Production and Inventory Control Society (APICS), American Society for Quality (ASQ), and Association for Manufacturing Excellence (AME). Drew is currently a faculty member at the Lean Enterprise Institute, and instructor for the National Institute of Standards and Technology Manufacturing Extension Partnership (NIST MEP).

www.cma4results.com

Books from Productivity Press

Productivity Press publishes books that empower individuals and companies to achieve excellence in quality, productivity, and the creative involvement of all employees. Through steadfast efforts to support the vision and strategy of continuous improvement, Productivity Press delivers today's leading-edge tools and techniques gathered directly from industry leaders around the world.

To request a complete catalog of our publications call us toll free at 888-319-5852 or visit us online at *www.productivitypress.com*.

Creating Mixed Model Value Streams:
Practical Lean Techniques for Building to Demand
Kevin J. Duggan

Creating Mixed Model Value Streams: Practical Lean Techniques for Building to Demand helps to address the challenges of high-mix manufacturing. The author uses a step-by-step approach, illustrated through a case study based on actual experience, to go beyond the basics of value stream mapping and show how to create future states in the real manufacturing world of multiple products, varying cycle times, and changing demand. The book includes a CD-ROM featuring useful spreadsheets for sorting products into families and calculating equipment needs. Comprehensive and down-to-earth, *Creating Mixed Model Value Streams* provides the details and new techniques for implementing lean in the complex environment that manufacturers face on their own shop floors.

ISBN 1-56327-280-6 I 2002 I 224 pages I Soft Cover I Stock # CMMVS-BK

Value Stream Management—Eight Steps to Planning, Mapping, and Sustaining Lean Improvements

Don Tapping, Tom Luyster, and Tom Shuker

Value stream management is a complete system that provides a clear path to lean implementation, ensuring quick deployment and great benefits. *Value Stream Management—Eight Steps to Planning, Mapping, and Sustaining Lean Improvements* shows you how to use mapping as part of a complete system for lean implementation. The central feature of this illustrative and engaging book is the value stream management storyboard, a tool representing an eight-step process for lean implementation. The storyboard brings together people, tools, metrics, and reporting into one visual document.

ISBN 1-56327-245-8 | 2002 | 175 pages | Soft Cover | Stock # VALUE-BK

Value Stream Management for the Lean Office—Eight Steps to Planning, Mapping, and Sustaining Lean Improvements in Administrative Areas

Don Tapping and Tom Shuker

Administrative functions represent up to 80 percent of the cost of doing business. Eliminating costly waste from administrative and office functions is a great way to increase your profit margin and a vital part of creating a total lean enterprise. Tapping and Shuker take their Value Stream Management Storyboard and apply its eight-step process in the context of a customer service case study based on an actual implementation. *Value Stream Management for the Lean Office* will provide you with a complete system for lean implementation in the office.

ISBN 1-56327-246-6 | 2003 | 176 pages | Soft Cover | Stock # LEOF-BK